ATHLETES
AND
ACQUAINTANCE
RAPE

SVAW

Sage Series on Violence Against Women

Series Editors

Claire M. Renzetti
St. Joseph's University

Jeffrey L. Edleson
University of Minnesota

In this series. . .

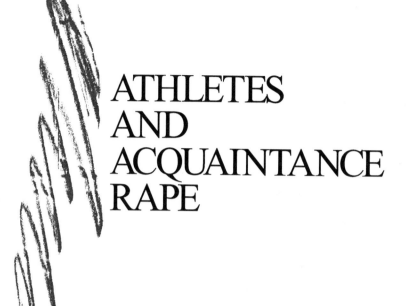

ATHLETES
AND
ACQUAINTANCE
RAPE

Jeffrey R. Benedict

Sage Series on Violence Against Women

SAGE Publications
International Educational and Professional Publisher
Thousand Oaks   London   New Delhi

For information:

SAGE Publications, Inc.
2455 Teller Road
Thousand Oaks, California 91320
E-mail: order@sagepub.com

SAGE Publications Ltd.
6 Bonhill Street
London EC2A 4PU
United Kingdom

SAGE Publications India Pvt. Ltd.
M-32 Market
Greater Kailash I
New Delhi 110 048 India

Printed in the United States of America

Library of Congress Cataloging-in-Publication Data

Benedict, Jeffrey R.
    Athletes and acquaintance rape / by Jeffrey R. Benedict.
      p. cm.—(Sage series on violence against women; v. 8)
    Includes bibliographical references and index.
    ISBN 0-7619-0966-4 (cloth: alk. paper).—
    ISBN 0-7619-0967-2 (pbk.: alk. paper)
    1. Acquaintance rape—United States—Case studies. 2. Athletes—United States—Sexual behavior—Case studies. 3. Rape—Investigation—United States—Case studies. 4. Trials (Rape)—United States—Case studies. I. Title.
II. Series.
    HV6561.B44 1998   97-45340
    364.15′32′0973—dc21

98 99 00 01 02 03 04 10 9 8 7 6 5 4 3 2 1

Acquiring Editor:	C. Terry Hendrix
Editorial Assistant:	Dale Mary Grenfell
Production Editor:	Astrid Virding
Production Assistant:	Karen Wiley
Typesetter/Designer:	Marion S. Warren
Indexer:	Trish Wittenstein
Cover Designer:	Ravi Balasuriya
Print Buyer:	Anna Chin

Contents

Acknowledgments

Long before deciding to write this book, a group of professors at Northeastern University expressed great support and interest in research I was conducting in conjunction with my graduate school studies. Professors Alan Klein, Eileen McDonagh, and Michael Tolley were enthusiastic about the potential impact of my work from the moment they learned of it. Their encouragement and insights went a long way to bring my research to the book stage. I am thankful for their friendship as well as their instruction and guidance.

This book would not have been possible without exceptional cooperation from medical personnel, defense attorneys, law enforcement officials, judges, defendants, and victims. I am particularly grateful to the Middlesex County District Attorney's office in Massachusetts; the County Prosecutor's office in Seminole County, Florida; personnel at the Middlesex County Superior Court in Cambridge, Massachusetts; personnel at the United States District Court at Seattle, Washington; the Rape Crisis Intervention Center at Beth Israel Hospital in Boston; and specialists at the Harvard Medical School.

I am particularly indebted to former assistant district attorney David Meier (currently the chief of the homicide unit in Boston) for his patience and tutoring, and to Massachusetts Superior Court Judge Robert Barton, who made his courtroom and his chambers a place of observation and first-hand learning. Likewise, I am appreciative of Honorable Walter T. McGovern and his resourceful clerk, Phil Lucid. Both allowed me to spend time in chambers.

I was also assisted in my research by attorneys who, despite their adversarial relationship in these respective cases, allowed me to visit their law firms to conduct interviews and review relevant documentation. The following were particularly helpful: Greg Garrison and his staff at Garrison & Kiefer in Indianapolis; Alan Dershowitz and his assistants at the Harvard Law School; Spencer Hall at Mundt, MacGregor, Happel, Falconer, Zulauf & Hall in Seattle; Byrnes & Keller in Seattle; Victoria Vreeland from Gordon, Thomas, Honeywell, Malanca, Peterson & Daheim in Seattle; and Howard Cooper from Hale & Door in Boston.

Although I did not rely too extensively on press reports, the reporting by Lynda Gorov of the *Boston Globe* and Tom Farrey of the *Seattle Times* was critical. Bold and able investigators, both granted me their time for questioning and background information.

Preface

In August 1995, prosecutors in La Crosse, Wisconsin, received a complaint alleging that numerous members of the New Orleans Saints football team sexually assaulted a woman in Sanford Hall on the University of Wisconsin campus where the team was being housed during its preseason summer camp. After a police officer in a patrol car spotted a woman crying outside the dormitory at a predawn hour, he approached her and asked if she was in need of help. The victim told the officer that she had been raped and held against her will by a number of Saints football players after having voluntarily accompanied a player to his room earlier that evening. A witness who had been outside the dorm moments before the victim emerged confirmed to the officer that she heard screams coming from the floor on which the Saints were staying.

The victim was shuttled to a nearby hospital for examination. Meanwhile, police investigators were dispatched to the dorm. They began by interviewing the two players staying in the room where the alleged incident took place. Once inside, the officers saw a pair of women's panties on the floor (the victim left her panties behind in her attempt to escape the room). Before police seized the panties as evidence, one of the players in the room began rummaging around in the area where the panties were located. He then asked permission to use the bathroom, and police discovered the panties were suddenly missing. The player was searched and the panties were discovered stuffed in his pants.

With the district attorney's office soon joining the investigation, a total of 30 players were interviewed. The players named by the accuser did not deny sexual contact. The following excerpt is from the prosecutor's report:

> Player 1 . . . and Player 2 did lie down and took their clothes off. . . . He [Player 1] stated that he and Player 2 did perform sexual intercourse with her and that she also had oral sex with him. He stated that at one point when she was having oral sex with Player 2 that he had sexual intercourse with her from behind. . . . When Player 9 entered the room . . . he took his clothes off and then attempted to put a condom on. . . . Player 1 stated that he specifically remembers seeing Player 5 standing in the doorway because he made the comment that he couldn't even get into the room with all the guys in there. ("Investigation Summary," 1995)

Nonetheless, after completing his investigation, prosecutor Ron Kind declined to press charges. "I believe that the credibility of the woman who reported the assaults would be insufficient to convince a jury beyond a reasonable doubt that the sexual contact she had with numerous players was not consensual," said Kind ("Declination Report," 1995). The decision appears callous and unjust in light of the players' conduct. Yet, Kind's decision is consistent with the growing trend among prosecutors to dismiss sexual assault charges against professional and college athletes for lack of evidence. Out of 217 felony complaints of sexual assault against athletes filed between 1986 and 1995, 100 were dismissed by law enforcement, primarily due to insufficient proof to surmount the hurdle of reasonable doubt. Of the remaining 117 that resulted in an indictment, 51 resulted in dropped charges or were pleaded down to misdemeanors (Benedict & Klein, 1997).

Dismissals and watered-down convictions are frequently met with harsh criticism by the media, women's groups, and victims' advocates. But the criticism has been inappropriately directed at law enforcement. It is the public that dictates whether athletes will be held accountable in these cases. Law enforcement's skittish approach to trying athletes for alleged acquaintance rape is predicated on jurors' unwillingness to convict athletes. Of the 66 athletes who were brought to trial on charges of rape during this time frame, only 6 were convicted (Benedict & Klein, 1997). Moreover, these 66 cases represented the cases with the strongest likelihood of a conviction (evidence of physical injury, timely reporting, strong victim, and in some cases multiple defendants—which would seem to refute the consent element). Thus, the inability to gain convictions even in these cases offers a clear illustration of the high esteem in which jurors hold athletes and the corresponding distrust of women who accuse athletes of abuse.

As in most acquaintance rape cases, conviction turns on the credibility of the accuser and the accused. When an athlete is the defendant, jurors are routinely faced with the question: Why would a famous athlete resort to force when he can have any woman he wants? Although both sexist and arrogant, this is the most natural defense for a powerful male celebrity to raise. This approach is often clever enough to fool jurors. Yet athletes' arrogant claims of having women readily available for their sexual desires raises a more relevant question: When celebrated athletes become so accustomed to having their sexual urges fulfilled on demand, are they capable of restraining themselves when confronted by a woman who says "no"?

With their power of self-restraint eroded by excessive sexual indulgence, many athletes become unwilling to accept rejection by women. Moreover, having never been held accountable by coaches, fans, the public, or the courts for ignoring a woman's wishes, there is little incentive for athletes to respect the word "no" from a woman. So why are jurors disinclined to convict famous athletes charged with sex crimes? In an attempt to answer this question, I have selected three cases—*Massachusetts v. Marcus Webb* (1993), *Victoria C. v. The Cincinnati Bengals* (1993), and *Indiana v. Mike Tyson* (1992)—that illustrate the problems associated with establishing violations of consent by athletes.

My conclusions are not based solely on these three cases. In addition, I researched more than 300 cases of alleged sexual violence involving athletes. Along with tracking the disposition of each complaint, I familiarized myself with the facts and circumstances of each case. This was accomplished by reviewing published reports, court documents, and, when possible, interviewing district attorneys, police, and defense attorneys directly involved in the cases.

Personal interviews were conducted with the professional athletes (defendants and teammates) where possible, as well as victims, defense lawyers, police investigators, prosecutors, presiding judges, jurors, and witnesses. Most interviews were recorded. In addition, I conducted many less formal interviews that were not recorded. Various court documents

(arrest warrants, police reports, affidavits, briefs, motions, jury instructions, evidence exhibits, testimony transcripts, court decisions, and appeals briefs) were also obtained and reviewed.

The choice of which three cases to feature was heavily influenced by
the willingness of the key participants in those cases to cooperate with
my research. I made telephone and written inquiries to attorneys and
other key players in over 50 cases in search of an affirmative willingness
to submit to interviews and make available necessary documentation to
thoroughly research the issues relevant to consent. The value of the
interview data is enhanced by the fact that not all court documents filed
in these cases are available to the public. Many of the critical memoranda,
briefs, and motions were filed under seal. I went through the presiding
trial judges, district attorneys, and defense attorneys to obtain the
overwhelming majority of court documents now in my possession. I
reviewed arrest warrants, police reports, official statements given to the
police by victims, affidavits, briefs filed by defendants and the state,
motions to admit evidence, motions to deny evidence, jury instructions,
trial testimony, court rulings, and briefs filed with the appeals courts.

Another reason for profiling the three cases I selected was the fact
that litigation had advanced far enough for the legal arguments to
develop fully. In other words, of the hundreds of cases that I reviewed,
many never got beyond the stage of a formal arrest. In order to fully
explore the use of the consent defense, it is necessary to have a case that
either goes to trial or advances to the stage where a trial date is set and
sufficient motions exist in the case file to provide an outline of the
defense's strategy.

Finally, I chose to chronicle these cases because most of the literature
treating the subject of athletes and sexual assault suffers from an absence
of primary source data. Scholars have produced a significant body of
anecdotal evidence suggesting an association between participation in
all-male, aggressive sports and the tendency to hold the belief that
women are inferior (Crosset, Benedict, & McDonald, 1995; Messner &
Sabo, 1994; Parrot & Bechhofer, 1991). A smaller body of data hints at
a link between membership on all-male athletic teams in revenue-
producing sports and sexual aggression (Crosset et al., 1995; Koss &
Gaines, 1993). But short of analyzing the attitudes and behaviors of
athletes on a case-by-case basis, it is merely speculative to link sports
participation with sex crimes. The deviant sexual practices of some of
today's celebrated athletes are a much stronger link to the sex crimes

they commit. Continuous engagement in sexual activity with random partners and the attitudes toward women that such conduct fosters are a much greater cause of athletes' abuse of woman than the mere fact of their athletic training. In short, the problem of rape by athletes is much more a result of their celebrity than their athleticism.

Introduction

The lion's share of rape complaints against athletes comes from victims who are socially acquainted with their perpetrator. Under these circumstances, as is the case in any complaint of acquaintance rape, proof beyond a reasonable doubt is difficult to establish. There are seldom any witnesses; physical evidence is usually sparse; and the cases are reduced to a he-said-she-said contest. But there are additional obstacles to a successful prosecution when the alleged perpetrator is a renowned athlete.

Ironically, athletes' increasingly deviant sexual habits are one of the most influential factors in insulating them from legal consequences when women accuse them of rape. Sexual indulgence has become a trademark of modern-day popular athletes. An increasing number of athletes publicly boast of rampant sexual promiscuity by themselves and their teammates (Barkley & Johnson, 1992; Bozworth & Reilly, 1988; Chamberlain, 1992; Johnson & Novak, 1992). The public's exposure to athletes' sexual practices has popularized the term "groupie," a label loosely applied to women who hang around athletes and often engage in sex with them.

Clearly, there are women who pursue athletes for sexual purposes. But groupie behavior (the pursuit of sexual relationships with famous athletes) is peculiar to an extremely small segment of women. Nonetheless, these women are a prevalent fixture in the social life of professional athletes. Moreover, their complicity reinforces the athletes' attitude of sexual license. In short, the jock-groupie tango is the engine driving the socialization process undergone by many athletes, which churns out an image of women as sexually compliant. The sex-for-fame commerce that exists between athletes and groupies undermines autonomy and trivializes the fundamental component of consent. Ultimately, athletes' indulgence in such relationships reduces their ability to distinguish between force and consent.

Whereas women who exhibit groupie behavior are certainly susceptible to victimization, an even greater threat exists for women who, despite having no explicit sexual interest in an athlete, come into social contact with a player and naively traverse consensual boundaries. Regardless of the circumstances, defense attorneys capitalize on the public's perception of groupies and generally categorize any woman who accuses an athlete of sexual misconduct as a groupie. Depicting the accuser as either a vengeful or fame-seeking groupie who has targeted a famous athlete invokes, at very least, the premise of implied consent. Defense lawyers seldom mention it, but the frequent sexual misconduct charges levied against athletes arise from a deviant lifestyle lived by some athletes that combines the lethal combination of being free from social responsibility and having unlimited access to random, consensual sexual encounters.

When an alleged incident of sexual violence occurs under these circumstances, neither a victim's claim of rape nor a professional athlete's plea of innocence is easily established. The obscurity of consent gives defense attorneys the upper hand, as their only task is to establish doubt in the minds of jurors. Prosecutors, on the other hand, must prove the use of force beyond a reasonable doubt.

Research on victim-rapist relationships reveals that rape is typically not an act of random violence, but rather exploitation of women who felt comfortable enough to be alone with their attacker (Parrot & Bechhofer, 1991; Russell, 1984; Warshaw, 1994). Attorney Susan Estrich, who popularized the term "simple rape," concluded that most rapes involving acquaintances are without signs of physical struggle, weapon use, or eyewitnesses. According to Estrich, the absence of corroborating evidence is used by defense lawyers as an indication that consensual sex occurred, as opposed to real rape (Estrich, 1987). Both court officials and jurors are receptive to rape myths because of pervasive stereotypes about female sexuality. Perhaps nowhere is sexual stereotyping more distorted than between athletes and women.

The influence of rape myths is a powerful diversionary tool. By injecting doubt, myths obscure the distinction between where voluntary action ends and coercion begins (Parrot & Bechhofer, 1991). Former New York City sex crimes prosecutor Alice Vachss pointed out that only two defenses are available to a defendant accused of acquaintance rape: "It never happened" and "consent" (Vachss, 1993). Athletes almost exclusively choose the latter.

The concept of consent is premised on physical power to act and free use of that power. But celebrated athletes have an unsurpassed combination of power and popularity, often placing the women who are with them on unequal ground from the outset. Former Los Angeles Laker Earvin "Magic" Johnson insisted that it is not unusual for women to offer their bodies for the pure sexual exploitation of professional athletes. As a result, some sports stars reach a point where they come to expect sex from all females who vie for their attention (Sherrington, 1994).

The expectation of sex that some athletes come to acquire is consistent with research suggesting that "rape-supportive attitudes are socially acquired beliefs" (Koss & Gaines, 1993). In 1988, Mary Koss conducted a survey of 2,972 men and found that "[m]ost men (88%) who reported an assault that met the legal definition of rape were adamant that their behavior was definitely not rape" (Koss, Gidycz, & Wisniewski, 1987). According to Gregory Matoesian (1993), this does not mean that all rapists are lying, "but rather that they may actually be more likely . . . to interpret sexual interactions as consensual, even if they involve various levels of physical force and coercion" (p. 5).

Much of the casual sex engaged in by athletes is seldom the result of affirmatively expressed consent or vocally conveyed resistance. Rather, there is a condition of sexual drift, or an instinctive flow toward sex, that is encouraged by the elevation of male athletes to cultural icons. Although much of the indiscriminate sexual activity participated in by professional athletes is the result of consent—thereby legally permissible—this atmosphere is nonetheless conducive to opportunities for felony rape.

Repeated sexual encounters with numerous partners narrows an athlete's view of women and convinces players that they can act with impunity toward any woman who vies for their attention. Mary Koss found that "the greater number of sexual partners a man has had, the greater the likelihood that he will have been sexually assaultive at least once" (Koss et al., 1987). In this context, a player may either engage in an act or acts that go beyond an acquaintance's will, or mistake a woman's behavior for what he views to be consistent with groupie behavior. Ensuing sexual advances clearly complicate matters.

The nature of these relationships and the subsequent circumstances surrounding a complainant's claim of being criminally violated present law enforcement officials with inherent obstacles that deter the likelihood of successful criminal prosecution. Rape statutes in most states define rape as "the unlawful carnal knowledge of a woman by a man forcibly and against her will." The courts consider a man's disregard for a woman's resistance to intercourse as a brutally violent act of commission, second only to murder in seriousness. Incidents of acquaintance and date rape, by definition, involve victims who knew their attacker and voluntarily agreed to be alone with him. Although such circumstances often provide a context for arguments of implied consent, rape laws make no allowance for men who presume privacy is a license for sex. Furthermore, most state statutes, including Indiana, Massachusetts, and Washington (the three states whose laws govern the cases featured in this book), stipulate that a woman maintains her autonomy to refuse intercourse even after she has engaged in other consensual acts of sex.

Whereas a woman's right to consent exists legally and socially in theory, it is often difficult to determine in practice where consent stops and force begins in situations involving two or more participants who have had previous sexual relations. As a general rule, accused athletes take special advantage of this circumstance and admit sexual contact while denouncing any implication of force. Defense attorneys buttress these claims by routinely denouncing almost all accusers as groupies.

When an athlete is identified as the perpetrator of a sex crime, prosecutors are typically confronted with an accuser who willfully accompanied the defendant to his bedroom, participated in some form of consensual activity—frequently sexual in nature—with the defendant immediately prior to the episode she describes as a rape, and may have even had associations with other professional athletes. Women who willfully enter into promiscuous encounters with star athletes compromise their autonomy once they enter a player's bedroom, whether it be a hotel or personal residence. In addition to the obvious fact that professional athletes are physically superior to most men—let alone women—professional players generally interpret a woman's willful entrance into their bedroom as a license to pursue their self-gratifying objectives with no concern for the acquaintance's desires.

Although women regularly enter and exit these brief sexual encounters without complaint, they are nonetheless susceptible to tremendous skepticism should they in fact become the victim of an assault. Under these circumstances, their consensual behavior preceding an incident of sexual assault subjects them to serious questions concerning credibility. As a result, women who are criminally violated in the bedrooms of professional athletes provide defense attorneys with character evidence that is potentially very persuasive in creating "reasonable doubt" in a juror's mind.

Furthermore, the prosecution is aware that the defense lawyers who will be bringing these facts to the attention of a jury are the most skilled and renowned litigators that money can buy, because of the considerable resources that professional athletes can muster for their defense. The superior skill of defense counsel is critical to these cases, due to the fact that rape cases are frequently absent of eyewitnesses. This fact compels the jury to ascertain the truth based on the believability of two opposing accounts of the same incident. Under this scenario, defense attorneys emphasize attributes of the accuser that undermine her credibility. Lawyers who represent professional players have the peculiar advantage of citing the unique social life of celebrity athletics, where there is an abundance of opportunity for illicit sex, as a reasonable explanation for implied consent.

Despite the victimization of women who had no desire for sexual involvement with their athlete-perpetrators, the circumstances of the athletes' subculture furnishes defense attorneys with a context to depict all accusers as groupies. The existence of groupie behavior exposes all victims of abuse to being branded a groupie.

The prevalence of groupie behavior provides a significant strength to the defense of professional athletes even in cases where the accused has exhibited no groupie behavior. Although the likelihood of successful criminal prosecution of felony rape charges is considerably enhanced when the prosecution can demonstrate to the jury that the accuser is not a groupie, the defense is nonetheless bolstered in its attempt to create reasonable doubt by associating the accuser with groupies.

A final, but no less important, issue complicating the prosecution of athletes for sex crimes is the race factor. There is often a racial overtone to many of these cases because of the high likelihood that an alleged athlete perpetrator will be black. For example, as of 1996, over 80% of the players in the NBA and nearly 70% of NFL players were black. Due to overrepresentation of blacks in professional sports, there is a corresponding overrepresentation of black athletes among the athlete-perpetrators. The shortage of white players in the ranks of celebrity athletics explains, in large part, the discrepancy between the number of white and black athletes being arrested for violating women. As further evidence of this point, Canada is seeing a growing number of its celebrity athletes being charged with violating women. A key distinction is that nearly all of the alleged perpetrator athletes in Canada are white males, a fact easily explained by virtue of hockey being the culture's top sport.

Despite the fact that race has no causal connection to men's abuse of women, defense lawyers and other supporters of the athletes will not resist raising racism as a motive for prosecuting players. Although there is rarely any basis to such accusations, the threat of being labeled racist serves to put law enforcement and others on notice to proceed with extra caution when investigating these matters.

These circumstances impede prosecutors when considering whether or not to present a case before a jury. As a result, district attorneys are frequently discouraged from seeking an indictment, or they are otherwise persuaded to entertain plea bargains more readily. It is rare for prosecutors to win a successful trial verdict in rape cases against professional athletes, due to the ease with which defense lawyers can portray victims as groupies. Jurors have proved to be too enamored, too trusting, and too forgiving of celebrated athletes who violate women.

1

The Subculture

Both the financial worth of professional sports franchises and the subsequent salaries being earned by professional players are astronomical. It is no longer uncommon for individual teams to exceed $200 million in value and for top players to be offered base salaries in excess of $4 million per year ("Athlete's High Salaries," 1993; "NFL's Top Dollars," 1995; Ozanian, 1993). The explosion in wealth associated with professional athletics is largely fueled by television contracts worth billions of dollars to professional leagues.

Because prime-time sporting events are unsurpassed in ratings, networks can attract millions of dollars in televised advertising during games. For example, the 1995 Super Bowl commercials cost $1 million per 30 seconds of air time (Horovits, 1995). In 1994, the Fox network agreed to pay the National Football League (NFL) $1.6 billion to broadcast 4 years of National Football Conference (NFC) football games for 19 weekends per year. Later in 1994, the National Collegiate Athletic Association (NCAA) reached an agreement with CBS wherein the network would pay $1.75 billion for the rights to televise college basketball games just in the month of March for the years 1995 through 2002 (Blum, 1995).

Due to the prevalence of organized men's sports on prime-time television, professional athletes have become virtually unsurpassed in their national popularity—particularly among teens and children. Seeking to utilize the mass appeal of sports personalities, leading advertising firms court professional athletes to endorse consumer products ("Converse Steps Up," 1995; "Fila Steps Up," 1995; "Super Bowl Ads," 1995). There now exists an entire industry devoted to packaging athletes as the commercial arm of major consumer products (Hudson, 1993; "Investors Bullish on," 1995). In addition to being the most sought after individuals for commercial advertising, it has become increasingly fashionable to see professional athletes appearing in movies, recording compact discs, and licensing their own products such as clothing and recording labels ("Pro Football Players," 1995; Rhoden, 1995; "Shaq Attacks Shaq," 1995). Even the publishing industry has turned to athletes to boost sagging book sales. Dennis Rodman's debut book, *Bad As I Wanna Be* (1996), reportedly sold 800,000 copies (Barnes & Noble representative, personal interview, May 5, 1997). Thus, while television has provided the means for teams to pay young athletes million-dollar salaries, it has played a more direct role in celebrity athletes transcending sports to become cultural icons in our society.

With billions of dollars contingent on the performance of today's professional athletes, players have become revenue-generating commodities. Modern-day athletes are fashioned into physical specialists designed to maximize their production on the playing field. The industry's competitive nature, which is fueled by financial incentives, converts high-priced athletes into investments. Any degree of absence from the field by a player diminishes a team's potential earnings. As a result, it is imperative to shield players from off-the-field responsibilities that detract from their ability to perform.

The formative stages of privilege bestowed on athletes begin in high school, progress during their collegiate years, and reach their apex as the athletes turn professional. For those few gifted young men who reach the elite level of professional competition, many are inclined to be socially irresponsible. With each advancement that a young man makes from high school to college to professional sports, he is incrementally relieved of tasks unrelated to his play and assured that he is exempt from the social norms. The gradual reduction in accountability climaxes in the awarding of a professional sports contract.

Athletes' exemption from accountability is further enhanced by the teams' acquiescence to their players' display of socially deplorable conduct. Even when players are associated with alleged criminal activity, management's vested financial interests compel them to refrain from imposing disciplinary action that will result in missed game time. Rather, teams will often extend their influence to assure the accused player's availability on game day ("Barnett Makes Most," 1994; Brubaker, 1994).

In addition to having unlawful conduct tacitly sanctioned by their employers, professional players surrender their domestic responsibilities to hired hands. The overwhelming physical demands often require 23-year-old professional athletes, most frequently without college degrees and work experience outside of sports, to use their exceptional wealth to hire agents, accountants, lawyers, and investors to manage their off-the-field affairs. Compartmentalizing professionalism implicitly separates sport from life and is underwritten by the sports work ethic according to which one maintains extreme discipline in the training for their sport, but behavior outside of sport is treated as leisure or downtime. Particularly during the playing season, a significant portion of idle time is spent in hotels, restaurants, theaters, nightclubs, and bars (Johnson & Novak, 1992). Thus, a curious reversal takes place in which the play world becomes real and the real world becomes play. Athletes often feel exempt from behaving responsibly away from the playing field. An NFL player adeptly described the following allegory to explain the profession of sports:

> Sports is a little boy's dream. That's what it is. It's a boy's game. Sports is for boys. When men engage in sport it's the ultimate job. Think about when you were a kid. If you could play marbles and make eighty grand a year playing marbles, "Wow." It's the ultimate job! The only other job as a kid that would probably be better than that would be watching cartoons. It's the same thing.
>
> What would you rather do on a Saturday afternoon when you had nothing to do? It was your day to make a decision: I'm either gonna [*sic*] play football or watch cartoons. You tell me that ten years from now that I can make money watching cartoons or play football, then I'm gonna watch cartoons—then probably play football.
>
> So it's a little boy's game that men have had a chance to play. It's a little boy's lifestyle that men have had a chance to do and make a lot of money doing it. So it's a little boy's dream that gets reinforced . . . there is a great deal of reinforcement. (personal interview, 1995)

One way of filling regular blocks of idle time available to athletes is to indulge in sex. One consequence of being a cultural icon is that pro athletes receive countless sexual offers from women who are drawn to their celebrity. The sheer volume of sexual encounters enjoyed by some professional athletes considerably reduces their ability to distinguish the intricacies of rape law that separate force from consent. Whereas it is common for accused sex offenders to insist on innocence, professional athletes do not plead innocence, they plead license.

When celebrity athletes who indulge in casual sex are faced with formal rape charges, their carefree lifestyle as a professional player suddenly collides with the extreme rigidity of the criminal justice system. In particular, the absolutism of the law's definition of sexual assault is applied to individuals who habitually participate in unrestrained sexual behavior. Accustomed to interpreting sex as merely routine leisurely conduct, accused players typically view the court proceedings with indifference and condescension.

High School

Young teenage boys who possess the rare physical talents necessary to become successful professional athletes find themselves receiving significant attention from adult figures. Recognizing particular abilities in young athletes, coaches and other authority figures invest unusual interest in an adolescent's potential to excel in a sport. Men will offer verbal encouragement, volunteer time to discuss ways of improving particular athletic skills, and even provide enticements to motivate a teenage athlete to work harder at a particular game. Such unnatural adulation from figures of authority conveys a message to a maturing teenager that he is uniquely entitled to preferential treatment that is unavailable to his nonathletic peers. "Athletics was what brought the attention," said one NFL player. "And being from an inner city school, when you do get notoriety it seems to come even bigger because the kind of attention I was getting other people wasn't getting" (personal interview, 1994).

Excellence in a sport distinguishes otherwise equal individuals from each other. Excessive notoriety at a young age is potentially destructive to any maturing adolescent. In the short term, the appeal of sport offers salvation—particularly to youth who are economically disadvantaged. The long-term consequence is particularly cruel to young men whose lives are otherwise devoid of positive reinforcement. The appeal of customized treatment from those who represent authority is very convincing. A former National Basketball Association (NBA) player recalled the following:

> All this stuff starts at age 13, 14, 15. A lot of these guys grow up poor. What happens when you come from nothing, or relatively nothing, once you're presented with something—in this case the natural, or unnatural, adulation that comes from adults patting you on the back or sliding you through classes, all that other stuff—you begin . . . to think that the world is handing out things to you. I mean they hand out praise. They hand out adulation because of your great basketball talent. (personal interview, 1994)

The allure of sport resides in the suggestion that excelling at the game can improve one's life chances. Young men from monetarily deprived backgrounds who are accustomed to having few material possessions are susceptible to the sport lure because it alone offers them the possibility of a reward. In time, they come to understand and comply with the reward structure. Psychologically, they learn that this singular gift is seized on by an ever-growing string of supporters. In short, fans see a dapper athlete and role model rather than an underprepared, postadolescent who cannot manage his college opportunities or grades.

The exceptionally gifted athletes have their notions of superiority reinforced by the practices of college recruiters. As early as their sophomore year in high school, players experience the pursuit of college coaches. Letters arrive from nationally renowned institutions whose sports teams are on television regularly. More important, the letters come affixed with a celebrity coach's name on the bottom. The abundance of letters and offers of scholarships virtually eliminates the motivation for a young teenager to excel academically in high school. Further, this practice instills complacency in many young children. With a guarantee to compete in college as a basketball or football player, 16-year-old boys have little encouragement to strive for academic perfection or to seek part-time jobs. An NFL player, who was a rape defendant, recalled the powerful influence that recruiting had on him:

> Recruiting for me wasn't like the kids in the private schools and even the suburban schools. Of course, these kids were always in the limelight. You always read about them. I guess

it was more rewarding for me. For me it was special because it was gettin' notoriety from kinda the pits, the bottom of the barrel so to speak. I was offered a scholarship pretty much any place I wanted to go. (personal interview, 1994)

College

For many basketball and football players, the transition from high school to college involves a drastic increase in the exposure of their talents. Although scholarship athletes are in the habit of being local heroes for their respective high schools, the hometown adulation pales in comparison to the multitudes of alumni, students, and local residents of the college town that support university teams. "I was from a big city but small school," an NFL player explained. "I had just never played in front of 100 people, never more than probably 75 people all through high school at home games. We're kind of an inferior program. We couldn't suit up 25 guys" (personal interview, 1994).

Suddenly, 18-year-old college freshmen are playing before tens of thousands of fans every week, and some of their games are even aired on national television. "The most shocking thing was the first game I suited up," the NFL player said. "I looked in the stands and there were 95,000 people" (personal interview, 1994). The enthusiasm for college athletics pushes young athletes to the pinnacle of popularity on their campuses. They are worshipped by students, adored by alumni, coddled by coaches, and often overlooked by professors who tolerate their pseudo-student status. "I used to walk around campus," said another NFL player, recalling his life as a college player. "I was the million-dollar guy. I was the Joe Montana of the state for a number of years" (personal interview, 1995).

The sudden rise in adulation is accompanied by both material and intangible rewards. First, athletes are cloaked with emblems that signify their unique status on campus. Colleges with Division I athletic teams furnish their scholarship athletes with matching, expensive name-brand tennis shoes and sweat suits. Segregated housing is reserved for athletes, sometimes luxurious in comparison to other student dormitories. Even private dining facilities complete with exceptional portions of food and fully catered meals are part of the scholarship package that athletes receive.

In addition to legitimate benefits that are an appendage to the sports scholarship, top players also receive other more ancillary monetary incentives. Restaurants and local businesses in the college community invite athletes to eat and select items without charge. Alumni will furnish players with cash, automobiles, and expensive off-campus apartments. "You had your car, whatever, you had your status," as one NFL player succinctly put it (personal interview, 1995).

These tokens of privilege are complimented by a systematic removal of typical college responsibilities inherent to student life. Players are spared the burden of selecting their own courses, registering for classes, purchasing textbooks, and returning their books at the close of a semester. Athletic departments deem these chores a distraction from game performance. Thus, coaches and team managers are employed to perform these tasks for the players. Although these simple responsibilities are an essential facet of the college experience designed to prepare students for adulthood, athletes are exempt. A defendant in the Bengals case explained,

> If you compared myself to a student that was just there on academic scholarships or grants or whatever, well what was the difference? The difference was he could work, I couldn't. We could come from the exact same background and exact same neighborhood. He had all the advantages and the only thing I had to hang my hat on was I was an athlete. Well, let's say I didn't make it to the next level. Well, the problem was that while I was so busy practicing he was busy studying. He was busy interviewing. He learned to write a resume. He had all the advantages on me. (personal interview, 1994)

In addition to the isolation from typical student responsibilities, athletes are also relieved from virtually all personal accountability as well. They are surrounded by individuals who do everything from calling them in the morning to ensure that they wake up on time, to carrying their luggage through airports on team trips. As citizens, student-athletes see their behavior condoned or overlooked when it violates either campus codes of conduct or local laws. Coaches and athletic administrators are often content to tolerate otherwise socially unacceptable behavior in exchange for superb athletic performances.

Combined, these factors convince college athletes that they are not subject to the same standards as their peers. Preferential treatment translates into entitlements. For college athletes who actually possess the skills to become a professional player, their time in school is merely a preparation for the professional game. Their treatment by the coaching staff, athletic administration, alumni, and student body is ample preparation for the absolute coddling they will receive on entering professional sports.

Knowing they are on the fast track to a professional sports career, stand-out college athletes frequently attach little or no importance to academic performance. Colleges are complicit in this by turning their heads while academically deficient athletes are permitted to continue playing (Benedict, 1997). As college coaches and administrators frequently acquiesce to preferential treatment for star athletes purely for selfish financial reasons, players learn that adherence to rules is contingent on athletic performance. The concept of accountability for one's off-the-field behavior is diluted in college and finally evaporates upon elevation to the professional level.

This experience effectively strips away all of their nonathletic identity and leads individuals to view student-athletes purely as athletes. In turn, the athletes also come to view themselves merely as athletes. Everything that a young athlete receives in terms of encouragement, entitlements, and support is based solely on his playing ability.

Coinciding with a narrowing view of the world around them, athletes' perceptions of women begin to constrict as well. Highly recruited athletes are exposed to women who are used to entice players to their school. This initial experience with women as a benefit is expanded over the course of a college career, and opportunities to bed coeds increase. Although women are commonly used as an enticement for luring players to school, as well as for retaining them once they accept a scholarship, the practice is not carried out by athletic-department employees. Instead, fellow athletes typically introduce recruits to women who are known to the players. One NFL player recalled,

> There were groupies in college—college groupies. Athletic department college groupies are usually ones that you meet on a recruiting trip. And they're there and they sleep with all the recruits, or they sleep with some freshmen. It's either someone that they [coaches and recruiters] are trying to entice

to come to the school or someone that's at the school and they want to keep happy. (personal interview, 1995)

Although this image of women is a gross distortion of the college coeds on campus, it is a perception that is increasingly reinforced over the duration of an athlete's college career. One NFL player described the common profile of the type of girl with whom athletes tend to associate:

A girl that sticks to the team and she supports the team. That's her deal. She wears a T-shirt to the game all the time and she's going to sleep with somebody that night. She's at the bar and she's there for whoever doesn't find somebody else, basically. (personal interview, 1995)

Although most college athletes manage to maintain other views of women besides the purely "college groupie" image, they are nonetheless being prepared for what is to follow on receiving a professional contract.

Professional

Any remnant of perspective that a college athlete may possess is eliminated when he signs a professional contract. Wealthy, 20-year-old athletes have their worldly affairs taken over by agents, accountants, and lawyers. This completes players' escape from social responsibility. Furthermore, unlike their high school and college experience, the professional sports ethic carries no pretensions such as education or compliance with school codes of conduct to distract the athlete. On the contrary, there is an overt dictum that prioritizes athletic performance over every other aspect of life. The release from all other concerns allows players to focus entirely on themselves as athletes. A former NBA player said,

I just don't know, given the pampered life of these kids especially nowadays. Even more so than their lives growing up—given the judgment they lack, the perspective they lack— because they've essentially been on scholarship. Even if they get to the pros at 21, for the last 7 or 8 years they've never had a chance to hit a brick wall in adolescence and really think about things that their actions could effect someone else.

> Because so much of their life—100% of it—is wrapped up in "me," which is all that sports is as an athlete, "How's it affecting me? What can I do to make 'me' better or get 'me' this?" (personal interview, 1994)

These problems are particularly acute for the rapidly expanding number of young athletes who are leaving college early or foregoing college altogether to enter the professional ranks. For example, in 1996, the NBA saw a record 42 underclassmen declare themselves eligible for the draft, including three high school players who opted to forego college altogether. There is every indication that these numbers will only continue to rise, increasing the occasion for millionaire adolescents to be thrust into a social environment that is replete with opportunities for illicit behavior.

Unprecedented wealth and endless adulation contribute mightily to a young professional athlete's perspective. Professional sports is one of the few industries that pays its highest salaries to the employees who have the least work experience. Due to the premium that teams place on securing young talent for extended careers, college players leave school and find themselves the recipients of instant wealth. Although endowed with lucrative financial contracts, players have little, if any, familiarity with finances because the NCAA prevents them from earning money while receiving a sports scholarship. Now earning anywhere from hundreds of thousands of dollars to millions of dollars annually, professional players are compelled to turn fiscal responsibility over to accountants and sports agents who manage their affairs. The inflated ego that often results from fame and fortune validates a lifestyle free from accountability off the playing field. One former NBA player explained,

> What society has done to our great athletes makes it very, very hard to maintain the perspective of the common man. You are dealing with some very, very uncommon men. Especially some of the backgrounds they come from. And they become, because of the nature of our sport in society, very uncommon citizens for the other way—for their great athletic skill. They are very uncommon because they are adored as an athlete. Probably no formal education and not a whole lot of social education either, which is even more important for getting

along in the world than the fact that they didn't get a bachelor's in history or something.

They've never had a mainstream life. You've got to understand that there is nothing in America like this. You can work for IBM or you can work for Mom and Pop Grocery store or anywhere in between, but if you are an athlete in America—and a very good one—there is nothing to compare your experience to other than Michael Jackson or something like that. (personal interview, 1994)

What begins in college as a steady stream of occasions to meet coeds becomes a cornucopia of sexual opportunity in the professional ranks of sports. Male professional athletes participating in high-revenue sports compose less than one tenth of 1% of the male population in the United States. There are less than 2,000 players in the NBA and NFL combined.

In addition to the wide popularity of professional athletes among male fans, there is a curiosity factor that attracts attention from many women as well. Whereas the overwhelming majority of women possess no desire for intimacy with an athlete, there is an exceptionally small yet constant presence of female sports groupies who pursue athletes for sexual purposes.

The meshing of these two narrow segments in the male and female populations forms a unique subculture, which has a primary purpose of providing both parties with brief and immediate indulgence in sexual gratification. "These groupies are sleeping around with several players," said one former NBA player. "And it's in every city. There's a cadre of women. Catch them as they come in, sleeping around with half the NBA" (personal interview, 1994).

The locations most frequently visited by athletes—nightclubs, bars, hotels, and designated restaurants—are where groupies gather. Both parties anticipate the other's presence, and sex is the implicit language between them. Existing in a social climate that facilitates random sexual encounters, professional athletes develop purely sexual images of women. One NFL player explained that when athletes either discuss women among themselves or meet women, sex is the foremost thought:

As an athlete you may meet someone, and she may be wonderful. It's happened to me on a few occasions where I've met women in different cities who I've gotten to know. You get to know them, and you talk to them. And then, all of a sudden, they say, "I know so and so." And you know him. And I go, "Oh man." And the first thing that comes to your mind is, "She's freaking."

"Freak" means she'll do anything. She'll do anyone, anytime, anywhere. She's a freak.

Or you'll be talking to a guy and say, "Yeah, I met so and so. I was in such and such a city, and I met so and so." And he goes, "Oh, you know her too?"

And he'll look at you and ask, "How was it? How was she?" (personal interview, 1995)

The integrity of consent is compromised in the context of "the meat market," where one is judged to have yielded all future autonomy on agreeing to accompany an athlete to his bedroom. Often, women who pursue professional athletes have engaged in sexual encounters with other athletes. Likewise, the athlete has experienced frequent sexual relations with other women. This tryst is mutually accepted because both parties are satisfying their distinctly different desires. Rather than clearly manifested consent, there is an occurrence of sexual drift or inferred gravitation toward sex that frequently culminates in sexual intercourse.

As a result, professional players perceive access to limitless sex as just another facet of the entitlements that accompany being a professional athlete. "The women are part of what comes with it," said an NFL player. "It's no different than the car. This [sex with women] is part of what comes with it" (personal interview, 1995). By reducing sex to a fringe benefit, women become mere objects for the pleasure of athletes. A former NBA player confirmed this:

> The same mentality hits with every other facet of your life. Comes down to women. Women are handing over their bodies to me. It's mine for the taking. They're there, why not? So you have the mentality of "Hey, it's not like I went out and roped her or grabbed her. She just presented herself on my lap." That's what I'm doing. That's sort of thinking with your loins and it's there and that happened. (personal interview, 1994)

The linking of celebrity athletes with women who exhibit groupie behavior epitomizes a disparity of power between the sexes. Whereas celebrity athletes have the opportunity for a plethora of sexual relations, women so inclined must surrender their autonomy before even gaining the companionship of a player. Thus, groupie behavior provides athletes with the availability of recreational sex, often without verbal conversation. An NFL player explained,

> Players indiscriminately will hump anything that slows down long enough for you to back up to it. When you're someone who has a lot of money and commands a lot of respect, you usually don't have to do anything. I know one guy who used to say, "If she ain't freaking, we ain't speaking," which meant "I don't even want to talk to you if you're not talking about going back to the hotel." (personal interview, 1995)

The abundance of sexual encounters experienced by athletes convinces some players that women enjoy succumbing sexually to professional players. Athletes' ability to classify women as leisurely possessions—available for the purpose of self-gratification and subsequent disposal—can be fully appreciated only by realizing that even married players have their promiscuity tacitly condoned by their wives. An NBA player explained,

> A lot of these guys get married pretty young. They have implicit deals with their wives that they're going to sleep around. The wives know it. The wives collect the income and maybe invest the checks and take care of the kids, stuff like that. It's a different fidelity than most grow up with—that once you have a wife, theoretically, you don't sleep around for whatever moral reasons or philosophical reasons, but a lot of times players get married young—maybe 20, 21, 22. They're in this atmosphere or environment where it's present all the time—the women. And a lot of times I think the wives put up with it. "I know he may be sleeping with these prostitutes. He's sleeping around with people who are less than women." And maybe they even accept it "as long as he's a good husband and doesn't beat me up and stuff like that." There are tacit agreements like that. It's almost a business deal. It's something I never wanted to deal with, which is probably why I said I would never marry while I was doing it. (personal interview, 1994)

The willingness on the part of players' wives to accept their husbands' promiscuity is peculiar. Nonetheless, it is a component in the marriages of some athletes. Consider the following statement from Magic Johnson's wife, Cookie, in his autobiography titled *My Life*, regarding his self-professed womanizing.

> When Earvin said he loved me, I knew he meant it, even when he was with other women. After I graduated from Michigan State, I spent eight years working in Toledo. I didn't expect Earvin to be a saint when I wasn't around. I had to face reality, and not live in a fantasy world like some women do. A lot of wives and girlfriends sit around and say, "Oh, my man would never do that." But most of them are kidding themselves. (Johnson & Novak, 1992, p. 250)

There are no available data on the attitudes of athletes' wives toward infidelity. But interviews with various players' wives indicate that Mrs. Johnson's tolerance of her husband's promiscuous ways is peculiar. Although some players' wives may naively believe that their husbands remain faithful, very few condone the kind of behavior described by Magic Johnson. However, the players believe they have license to cheat on their wives with impunity. Magic's wife added:

> When you're talking about Earvin and women, the first thing you have to understand is that Los Angeles is a big part of the story. . . . It's almost like Earvin can split himself into two people. . . . Showtime [the nickname for the Lakers' fast-break style of play] wasn't just on the court. Part of the show was all those gorgeous women walking around the Forum, on display. And the players noticed. Definitely. They'd be at the free-throw line, and on the bench, and they'd look, too. They'd start thinking, Well, I guess this is mine for the taking. And they were right. I'm amazed they were able to be so discreet about it.
>
> No wonder Earvin took so long to get married. He didn't want to let go of that world. What man would? (Johnson & Novak, 1992, pp. 260-261)

Although such indiscriminate sexual behavior may conflict with society's norms, this sexually deviant lifestyle is not criminal. However, such frequent participation in one-night stands erodes a player's ability to discern consent and ultimately facilitates opportunities for incidents of rape. Rapes occur when athletes either fail to recognize a woman who merely desires the social company of a celebrity, or when players refuse to respect a woman's right to refuse certain acts of sex—particularly if a woman has consented to a previous sexual act. Accustomed to being pursued by women who exhibit groupie behavior, some athletes form sweeping generalizations about all women and sex. An NBA player explained,

> I'm not sure, given the opportunities that players who want to partake in voluminous sex—one night stands—players can tell the difference anymore. You've been to bed with so many, can you clearly define what you think is consent or what someone else thinks is rape? It's just become so natural and happenstance to you. Given the mentality of these guys and given the relative lack of perspective, I'm not sure they could ever discern the difference between consent and force. (personal interview, 1994)

Contrary to the perceptions of many athletes, a significant number of women are more concerned with the self-satisfaction that comes from notifying their friends and family of their brief social encounter with a famous celebrity. A former NFL player said,

> Even women who aren't groupies have a fascination with athletes, especially professional athletes. If she's in a circle with an athlete, this has happened to me many times, she knows nothing about sports, but that guy that she's with or her husband or her boyfriend or her father, whoever, says, "This is [name deleted]. Don't you know who he is? Let me tell you something about this guy." And he raves and raves and raves and raves and raves.
>
> So even the ones who don't even look at it that they're professional athletes, it's how they're reacted to by the people. It's how they're treated by the people, the people who they [the women] trust and know. (personal interview, 1995)

Irrespective of whether a woman knows the particulars of the sport he plays or who he is, the fulfillment results from associating with someone who is adored by the general population. An NFL player explained,

> There are the girls who you meet by chance who are thrilled with the fact that they're talking to someone that everyone else thinks is important. It's not so much that they think you're important, but everyone else thinks you're important. (personal interview, 1995)

The Incident

The suggestion of a woman accompanying a player to his room for anything other than sex is altogether contrary to an athlete's everyday experience. There are two common scenarios wherein professional athletes generally commit acquaintance rape. Under the first scenario, it is more difficult to distinguish the presence of consent. Typically, under this pretext, a woman initially makes herself available to an athlete and may even participate in some form or forms of consensual sexual activity. Despite willful entrance into previous casual sex, she is either unprepared or unwilling to participate in a particular act that a player desires. This may include oral or anal intercourse or allowing additional teammates to join in. Her complicity in previous sexual activity causes the athlete to take license and disregard any communication designed to stop his advances.

Under the second rape scenario, consent and force are more clearly distinguishable, yet no less difficult to prove in court. For example, a woman who displays eagerness to gain association with a famous celebrity is easily perceived as a groupie by some athletes, leaving players to presume sex as the motive. Despite a lack of sexual overtures on the woman's part, the mere fact that she willingly accompanied a player often triggers consent in the athlete's mind. Under these circumstances, even a subsequent clear refusal by the woman to engage in sex is likely to be disregarded. "It goes back to what you're conditioned to," said one NFL player. "When you're used to getting your own way, you don't understand the other alternative" (personal interview, 1995).

The mental-training regimens that accompany revenue-generating sports provide another factor at work in these situations. The mental edge needed to win at the highest levels of competitive sports can have dangerous repercussions for women when misapplied by some athletes. One NFL player explained that the self-denial required to survive in professional athletics is consistent with a player's ability to deny a woman's resistance to sex.

> Before I go into something I have to pump myself up so that I know that I can't be beat, and then you go into it with confidence. You talk about sex as casual sex, as a recreation, as a conquest—why would your attitude be any different when you approach it that way? It's very congruent with the way athletes live in so many other ways. (personal interview, 1995)

Athletes lie when convincing themselves that they can conquer any opponent—even those who are far superior. Likewise, some athletes lie to themselves when a woman rebuffs their sexual advances.

A player's dismissal of a woman's clear communication of "no" satisfies the legal definition of force. Professional athletes are prime candidates to commit the crime of rape because of their entrenched belief that even women who say "no" in fact mean "yes." An NFL player explained,

> They say, "Well, she probably doesn't want to, but I'm so good she's gonna love this." Because that's what you tell yourself. Because you lie to yourself about how good you are in what you do. If you have to go up against Michael Jordan, you're going to tell yourself, "I can play Michael Jordan." You have to because the minute you doubt yourself, you're done. He's by you. (personal interview, 1995)

Whereas the sport subculture fosters images of women as sexually compliant, and simultaneously facilitates opportunities for players who may possess proclivities toward sexual abuse to be pursued by women, sport also offers a final factor that fuels the perception that athletes are not accountable, regardless of how they treat women. As the cases that follow will illustrate, sport enables sex offenders who are athletes to be supplied with superb legal counsel without exerting any effort what-soever. Rather, teams and player agents assemble legal defense teams and use the players' wealth to finance the lawyers. Further, the built-in attraction of the press to celebrity-athletes provides a platform for high-profile attorneys to defend their clients long before court is in session. These factors sour victims' appetites for enduring the length of a trial and impede the efforts of prosecutors to successfully indict and prosecute athletes. The failure to convict athletes of felony rape only enhances their perception of license and further fuels their proclivity toward treating women in a degrading way.

2

Massachusetts v. Marcus Webb

After dropping out of college and being passed over by NBA teams in the 1992 college draft, Marcus Webb earned the last spot on the Boston Celtics roster during a summer tryout. Despite being the lowest paid player on the team, he nonetheless wore the famous Celtics uniform and played alongside Larry Bird and other famous players. Webb immediately immersed himself in the social high life afforded NBA players, becoming a regular at Boston's night clubs that were notorious for attracting Boston-area athletes. In the company of other Celtics players, he was frequently approached by women.

Overwhelmed by the instant adulation, Webb engaged in sexual relations with as many women as possible. A Boston-area college student, who previously had relations with another Celtic player, pursued Webb and began sleeping at his apartment regularly. She accepted, without argument, the fact that he was sexually active with other women.

On Friday, March 3, 1994, Webb and the college coed participated in various sex acts at his apartment prior to the Celtics game against the San Antonio Spurs. That same day, Webb had informed her that their brief relationship was over due to his intention to reestablish relations with a former girlfriend who was also the mother of his child. After attending his game, Webb went out with some of his teammates before returning home. Sometime after midnight, he returned home and unexpectedly found the coed still at his apartment. According to prosecutors, he perceived her presence as an opportunity for one last sexual fling. The victim claimed she was flipped over onto her stomach and forcibly raped anally.

Suffering severe tearing and abrasions around the anal opening, the victim entered Boston's Beth Israel Hospital and later pressed charges against Webb. He was arrested and charged with first-degree felony rape.

The defense attempted to introduce evidence of the victim's sexual history with other Boston-area athletes, as well as countless letters she wrote to Webb. Prior to the judge's ruling on the admissibility of evidence regarding the victim's background, the district attorney's office agreed to a plea bargain that reduced Webb's charges to third-degree sexual misconduct, and he was sentenced to serve 30 days in jail.

The Profile

High School

Marcus Lataives Webb grew up in a single-parent home in a poor section of Montgomery, Alabama. Although fathered by former University of Alabama football star George Pugh, Webb was raised solely by his mother. As she was often forced to work three and four jobs to support them, Marcus was left to the guardianship of other relatives. At an early age he developed unusual physical size and by his twelfth birthday, both his height and weight caused him to stand out among his classmates.

His superior physical attributes attracted the attention of both junior high and high school coaches. He was pursued by the coaches at the junior high in an effort to convince him to play for the school's sports teams. "Sports discovered me in 7th grade," Webb told *Boston Globe* reporter Lynda Gorov. "They didn't ask me to play football; they told me" (Gorov, 1993c).

Even before reaching high school, others observed that Webb "sensed the privilege that accompanies athletic prowess" (Gorov, 1993c). While attending Sidney Lanier High, he established himself as an all-state basketball and football player. Sports quickly began to define Webb's perception of himself and to occupy much of his time. "In football, I was Mr. Everything," boasted Webb. "Basketball, Mr. Everything. Track, Mr. Everything" (Gorov, 1993c).

Coinciding with his exceptional success on the playing field, he was exhibiting little interest in school. Although Webb's classroom deficiencies were shared by other students, he alone was elevated to a position of schoolwide popularity and catered to by his coaches and teachers because of his promising athleticism. The exceptions that were made for Marcus coincided with his fundamental stage of development as a teenage adolescent. The recognition by admiring adults for his physical gifts put Webb on an accelerated track to a career in sports by the time he neared the end of his high school years. Excelling in three high school sports, Webb became convinced that everything was secondary in importance to his athletic performance; thus, commitment to his studies was virtually absent.

Former high school teachers and coaches attributed poor performance in the classroom to his "trouble with responsibility" (Gorov, 1993c). A former high school teammate of his suggested, "He never did understand how to manage his time and his money" (Gorov, 1993c). The high school's Reserve Officers' Training Corps (ROTC) director, Col. Charles Scott, convinced Webb to join the reserves in an effort to instill some responsible behavior, yet there was little motivation for Webb to change his ways, because he was being pursued by major colleges with scholarship offers to play sports. As Scott admitted, "It was tough for him to see the serious side of things" (Gorov, 1993c). In his senior year, Webb accepted a full scholarship to play basketball at the University of Alabama, the state's most prestigious sports institution.

College

After enrolling at Alabama, Webb, along with his teammates, was provided with tutors employed specifically to compensate for the extensive hours required for practice and games. The coaching staff encouraged Webb to sustain some semblance of grades in order to maintain his playing eligibility, but they provided little incentive for him to take their requests seriously. Despite having the disposition to skip classes and avoid handing in assignments, Webb remained eligible to play in all Crimson Tide basketball games.

Meanwhile, Webb's irresponsible behavior began to expand beyond the classroom and into the community. While playing for Alabama, he was arrested twice and collected enough speeding tickets to cause the state of Alabama to suspend his license. It was later revoked when he was caught speeding with a suspended license. Although the state of Alabama imposed various fines, temporary incarceration, a suspended sentence, and probation on Webb, his legal troubles triggered no substantial team disciplinary action. Instead, his eligibility to participate in the school's basketball games continued uninterrupted.

Coinciding with run-ins with the law and failing grades, Webb's popularity among the women on campus continued to rise due to his presence on the basketball team. Before leaving Alabama, he was responsible for impregnating Quientina Brown, and he became the subject of a paternity suit filed by LaTangelia Sanderson, who insists that he also fathered her child (Ranalli, 1993).

Prior to the start of Webb's senior season, head coach Wimp Sanderson—himself the subject of a sexual harassment suit stemming from the abuse of his secretary—summarily suspended Webb from the team. Sanderson insisted that he "couldn't tolerate him not going to class [and] being behind in his schoolwork" (Gorov, 1993c). This action came only after Webb spent 3 years failing to exhibit any interest in school outside of basketball, having repeated violations of the law and incidents with women. Upon suspension from the basketball team, Webb promptly dropped out of college and pursued a professional career in basketball.

Professional

Following a brief stint in the United States Basketball League, Webb's 6'9", 255-lb frame attracted various inquiries from NBA teams, and he was eventually invited to attend a camp sponsored by the Boston Celtics. At the conclusion of the summer of 1993, he was offered a 1-year, $150,000 contract to play professional basketball. After growing up in a depressed section of Montgomery, having little more than a high school education and no formal job experience, Webb received his first significant paying job at age 22. Overnight, he became one of just 12 members of the most storied basketball franchise in the country.

While enrolled at the University of Alabama, Webb was expected to maintain the appearance of being a student in addition to playing basketball. As a professional, he was awarded an unprecedented salary to devote his energies exclusively to basketball. Even before Webb secured the contract, he began to experience newfound attention from the press and the fans who chronicle the lives of the players as much as they do the games. Reporters wanted his opinion, and men, women, and particularly children wanted his autograph.

Just months after Webb's first NBA season began with the Celtics, he was involved in a well-publicized incident involving law-enforcement officials in Boston as a result of his repeated inability to arrive on time for scheduled team practices and appointments. With a number of "late arrivals" on his short record of employment with the Celtics, Webb failed to appear at a scheduled medical appointment with the team physician and a subsequent team practice on January 8, 1993. When confronted by Celtics officials regarding the missed appointments, Webb concocted a fictitious account of being pulled over without just cause by a group of white police officers from two neighboring Boston suburbs, being detained for over an hour along the highway, and finally having one officer confiscate and rip up his State of Alabama temporary license before releasing him. Due to the city of Boston's storied history of racial incidents, Webb's allegations exposed the accused police departments from the suburban towns of Newton and Brookline to instant public scrutiny. Furthermore, well-documented cases of far more popular black athletes encountering overt racism in Boston compelled the media to investigate the actions of the accused law-enforcement officials (Fainaru & Murphy, 1993; Shaughnessy, 1993).

The pending investigation into Webb's account revealed that the State of Alabama had never reissued him a temporary license after revoking it for repeated driving violations. Thus, he had been violating Massachusetts driving laws for the entire time that he had been driving his brand new jeep, since shortly after signing his contract. Further, his report of being pulled over by an officer named "Smith" was disproved when it was discovered that neither of the departments included in Webb's allegations employed an officer by that last name. The truth revealed that Webb carelessly subjected the integrity of two entire police departments to scrutiny by linking the officers with inflammatory charges of racism—all in an attempt to cover for his failure to appear for work on time. Nonetheless, the Celtics chose not to impose any disciplinary action on Webb. Further, there was no public apology offered to the police officers and towns falsely implicated in this tale. Rather, the team fined Webb $150 for missing morning practice and $100 for missing a doctor's appointment. Even while the mayors and police chiefs from both towns publicly demanded an explanation and clarification for the actions of Webb, he conveniently hid behind the Celtics reputation as it was criticized by the press for failing to admit that Webb falsely discredited law enforcement officials.

The money invested in Webb insulated him from liability for his irresponsible behavior. It was further evidence to Webb that he was not subject to the same rules as the rest of society as long as he was wearing a Celtics uniform. Massachusetts Superior Court Judge Robert Barton, who presided over the subsequent rape case against Webb, confirmed that there was a direct correlation between Webb's conditioned attitude of "Well, I'm a Boston Celtic. I can get away with this type of thing," and the events that unfolded in his bedroom between him and the woman who accused him of rape. Barton stated,

> The athletes are spoiled. They're pampered. Many of them don't have the inner discipline. Even though they have the inner discipline as athletes, they don't have the inner discipline to comport their behavior to what society expects. They've been spoiled everywhere they've gone. Everybody has covered for them. The coach has covered for them. The professors have covered for them. The police cover for them . . . to make sure that the star quarterback or basketball player or baseball player is going to be able to play next week. (personal interview, 1994)

The Access

Coinciding with this absolute elimination of responsibility for actions away from the basketball court came the challenge of going from a small rural town in Alabama to being a celebrity in a big city. At age 22, Webb's membership in a fraternity of young, rich basketball bachelors expanded his access to adoring women. He immediately joined four or five other Celtics in nightly appearances at the most fashionable Boston-area clubs and bars. Due to the tremendous physical size of professional athletes, the mere presence of these players attracted the attention of everyone. Webb's defense attorney, Howard Cooper, observed,

> It is striking how large of a guy Marcus Webb is. And I imagine that's true with respect to all basketball players. Until you are in a room with these guys you just don't realize how big they are. I know football players are big guys, but basketball players really tower above people. And as a result, when Marcus Webb or his teammates go out to a bar they can't fade into the woodwork. They are just there. I have to imagine that in a bar, where it's a singles event and people are there to meet

each other, that clearly is a factor. He clearly stood out. (personal interview, 1994)

In addition to his physical size, Webb's face had become one of the most well known in the city of Boston. Although he was the lowest paid player on the team and rarely received any playing time, his social circle was an elite group of young superstars. "There's only 12 guys on the Celtics roster," Cooper explained. "And basketball is king in this town. Everybody knows who all the Celtics are. So not only is he a very large man, but he is a face that is well known" (personal interview, 1994).

The clubs were the most consistent form of leisure entertainment for Webb and a select group of teammates. Typical days consisted of 3 to 4 hours dedicated to basketball and a nightly appearance at a bar or nightclub to socialize, dance, and meet women.

Webb and his small association of teammates had their elite social circle joined by an equally exclusive group of women who were typically young, well-dressed, physically attractive girls who preferred sports celebrities. According to Cooper, the pretrial investigation interviews with other Celtic players revealed that their social group involves

a different subset of women—that is, the same group of women shows up to every bar. And that there's a different bar for different nights of the week. Different clubs. And that the women are just always there looking to meet professional athletes. (personal interview, 1994)

Although Webb had been the recipient of a fair amount of attention from coeds while playing college basketball at the University of Alabama, he was clearly unprepared for the aggressive pursuit of female devotees pending his signing of an NBA contract. At Alabama, he was without a large contract and he was seldom on television. In Boston, he represented the often aspired to lifestyle of the young, rich, and famous. In the clubs, he was the recipient of attention from women who would submit to him sexually simply because of his status. Webb clearly was not prepared for the dramatic increase in attention from women whom he encountered in clubs. He stated, "Northern women are a hell of a lot different, more wild and loose. Once, in a club, a woman tried to undress me on the dance floor. I couldn't believe it" (Gorov, 1993b).

Webb quickly learned that employment as an entertainer was accompanied by the limitless availability of casual sex. With the sudden awarding of unprecedented money, popularity, and adulation, women took the form of just another entitlement. His attorney described the following:

> In his newfound status as a Boston Celtic, he was out there dating a lot of women and he was one of the young, single Celtics who was regularly in attendance at the clubs. And there was constantly a lot of women following him and calling him. And he was enjoying that a lot. I don't want to make him seem entirely base—that he was just out there trying to screw anything that moved. He was actively participating in the Boston social life. (personal interview, 1994)

Existing in a very limited environment that consisted of playing in the Boston Garden, traveling to play in other cities, and partying in the clubs and bars, Webb adopted the unique attitude toward women and casual sex that is shared by those players in the NBA who take advantage of the limitless opportunities for sex. As Cooper explained,

> Pro athletes are these young guys who have the attitude that the world is their oyster for plucking. They're young, generally in their early twenties. They have money. In Marcus Webb's case, for the first time in his life he had some money. There's an attitude out there that this is just a woman who is known to hang out with pro athletes and be available for them sexually. And that's the way of the world—their world. (personal interview, 1994)

One NBA player confirmed that players translate the unnatural adulation that comes from adults—patting you on the back or sliding you through classes—into every other facet of life, particularly in relation to women (personal interview, 1994). Judge Barton added,

> The females at these places [nightclubs frequented by professional athletes] throw themselves all over these ball players. So the players can't believe that anybody would ever say "No"

to them. They are spoiled as men because you have women throwing themselves all over you. So after awhile, you begin to believe that you personally are something special. (personal interview, 1994)

One woman who pursued Marcus through the club scene was Emerson College student Ericka Gomes. She had previously dated other Celtics. After being introduced to Webb, Gomes became one of the women with whom Webb was routinely engaging in casual sex.

Before meeting Webb, Gomes had participated in an extended sexual relationship with another member of the Celtics who was traded prior to Webb's arrival. She was quite familiar with the sexual practices of professional athletes and numerous Celtics were likewise aware of her fetish for professional athletes. Assistant district attorney David Meier, who subsequently prosecuted Webb, verified that "when she got involved in a relationship with Webb, she knew or believed that Marcus Webb was going out with other women" (personal interview, 1994).

Despite her knowledge of Webb's sexual involvement with other women, Gomes frequently slept at Webb's apartment and willfully participated in a very active sexual relationship with him. As the frequency and intensity of their interaction increased, Meier explained that Gomes openly discussed her relationship. "The victim told her friends how much she was in love with Marcus Webb and how happy she was with Marcus Webb," said Meier (personal interview, 1994).

Howard Cooper added, "She had discussed, in graphic detail and in a joking-around manner, how good the sexual relationship with Webb was" (personal interview, 1994). During the 6-week relationship, Webb received intimate letters from Gomes that indicated her love for him. Webb, on the other hand, was aware that Gomes was labeled a "freak" among some players. The term "freak" is common jargon among professional athletes to describe a woman who is attracted to athletes and available for sex. Clearly, this is the perception that Webb had of Gomes. Cooper said that one of the key witnesses prepared to testify at trial used the word "freak" to describe Gomes during his affidavit. Based on his interviews with other Celtic players, Cooper concluded, "it [freak] was a word that I would assign to someone who was available—that she likes athletes" (personal interview, 1994). To Webb, Gomes was available for sex upon convenience, whereas Gomes was fantasizing about a nonexistent love affair.

The Incident

In late February 1993, Marcus had received word that the mother of his child in Alabama, Quientina Brown, was coming to Boston. During his college days, they had a serious relationship that broke off before he left the state. In preparation for her visit, Webb insisted that Gomes, who had been sleeping in his bed regularly, vacate his apartment. "Marcus told Gomes, for all intents and purposes, the relationship was over," insisted Cooper (personal interview, 1994).

On March 3, the Celtics were scheduled to play a home game against the San Antonio Spurs. On game days, players are not required to be at the arena until nearly 6:00 in the evening, thus leaving a significant amount of daytime hours with nothing to do. Webb and Gomes spent part of the day at his apartment listening to music. Furthermore, they participated in a significant amount of consensual sexual activity including intercourse. Late in the afternoon, he was picked up by one of his teammates and driven to the Boston Garden, while Gomes remained behind at his apartment.

Webb did not dress for the game due to a thumb injury. Instead, he sat on the bench in street clothes. The game was over before 10:00 and Webb joined a small group of his teammates who went out to dinner and then visited various bars. Finally, a teammate dropped Webb off at his apartment after midnight. Gomes was still at his residence and the two of them proceeded to engage in casual sex again.

While participating in what began as consensual sex, Webb flipped Gomes over and initiated anal intercourse. "[He] forced her down on the bed and forced her face into the pillow," according to assistant district attorney James Takacs ("A Tangled Web," 1993).

At the conclusion of the incident, she retreated to another room and remained there until morning. After waking, she placed two phone calls before leaving the apartment and admitting herself to the rape crisis center at Beth Israel Hospital, less than 12 hours after the incident took place. The rape examination revealed significant abrasions, tears, and bleeding in and around the anal opening.

The following day, March 5, the results from the rape kit were forwarded to local police. On March 6, Gomes contacted the Middlesex County district attorney's office and reported the incident. On March 7, while the district attorney's office began to investigate the rape allegations by Gomes, Webb and his former girlfriend from Alabama were involved in a dispute that spilled over into violence. He ended up assaulting Quientina Brown in his apartment and she called the police.

Four days later, Webb and Gomes met at the Harbor Club, a prominent Boston-area nightclub, to reconcile their differences. That escalated into a physical altercation in which Gomes claimed that "Webb yanked her hair and grabbed her hard enough to leave a bruise the size of his palm on her upper arm" (Gorov, 1993a). Later that evening, he allegedly came to her home at 3:30 in the morning and "picked her up and threatened to throw her off the balcony" (Gorov, 1993a). This resulted in Gomes obtaining a restraining order against Webb on March 15, the same day the police arrested him and charged him with assault and battery in the Brown incident.

Meanwhile, the district attorney's office collected sufficient evidence to issue a warrant for his arrest on the rape charge. On March 18, the police arrived at Boston Celtics practice facilities, located on the campus of Brandeis University, and arrested Webb for the rape of Gomes. That same day, the Celtics waived him, leaving Webb incarcerated and without a job.

The Court's Response

Jurisdiction

After the grand jury proceedings and some preliminary hearings, the case was assigned to one of Middlesex County's most experienced prosecutors, David Meier. The publicity surrounding the allegations and subsequent arrest of a Boston Celtic was a clear indication that "this [was] not going to be your garden variety rape case," said Meier (personal interview, 1994).

Meier confirmed that athletes accused of sexual assault typically have legal counsel that far exceeds that of most defendants charged with rape, and their cases are handled in a different manner. Prosecutors who indict professional athletes inherit unique obstacles in rape cases. Most notable is the knowledge that the state will be opposed by the best counsel that money can buy. "Athletes receive the best defense available because these people have resources and . . . because the public has held these people up to higher esteem than the guy in the alley," said Meier. "There are definitely inherent obstacles in these types of cases" (personal interview, 1994).

Assembly of Lawyers

After Webb's arrest, the Boston Celtics were influential in the decision by the prestigious Boston law firm of Hale & Dorr—which represents the Celtics in legal matters—to dispatch an attorney to handle Webb's arraignment. Meanwhile, Webb's sports agent flew home from Israel for the purpose of conducting interviews with prospective legal counsel to represent Webb for the duration of the case. The Celtics' attorneys recommended J. Owen Todd, a former state superior court judge, and his partner, Howard Cooper, and they were subsequently retained as defense counsel.

It is common for athletes accused of rape to be represented by notable lawyers who are extremely competent and high priced. Nonetheless, these attorneys typically have little if any experience in litigation involving sexual assault. Only about 10% to 15% of Todd and Cooper's practice is criminal defense work, primarily white-collar crime and drug and gun cases. "I can't recollect," said Cooper, "since we started this firm, doing another rape case" (personal interview, 1994).

Todd and Cooper were retained not because they had lengthy experience representing accused sex offenders, but because they are very talented lawyers experienced at trying cases that involve high stakes. "People who have money can afford the best lawyers," said Judge Barton, who previously served on the bench with Todd. "J. Owen Todd's a former superior court judge. He knows what he's doing. He's a high priced lawyer. The average fellow who is charged with rape can't afford a lawyer" (personal interview, 1994).

The Athlete's Perception
of the Incident

After being released on bail, Webb insisted that he did not want Gomes to drop the charge against him because he wanted vindication in court. "[Sex with Gomes] wasn't a one-time thing," Webb stated publicly. "After all this embarrassment, it's going to trial. I'm not going to jail" (Gorov, 1993b).

Gomes was in a significantly inferior position to Webb when he made up his mind to have his way sexually with her. Having continually gone to his apartment and willfully engaged in acts of sex, she compromised her ability to accuse him of using force. Meanwhile, she was well aware that other women were making themselves available to Marcus as well.

Judge Barton offered the following observation regarding the disproportionate division of power within the Webb-Gomes relationship:

> The more power people have—be they athletes or be they
> politicians—they feel that they're above the average human
> being and, therefore, they can get away with more. They have
> more control. They have more power. Athletes are in posi-
> tions of power. Monetarily they are in a position of power.
> But also, as far as hero worship, they are in a position of
> power. I'm sure the last thing that Mr. Webb ever thought was
> that this woman would ever make a complaint against him.
> (personal interview, 1994)

One former NBA player suggested that the type of access to women
afforded Webb and other NBA players obscures the concept of consent
because there is such a prevalence of opportunities to participate in
relationships that have no constraints and no purpose other than to
gratify the two participants. "Players who are sleeping around or who
have the women thrown at them . . . don't even understand or comprehend consent, given the opportunities . . . to partake in voluminous
sex and one night stands," the former player said (personal interview,
1994).

Despite the significant advantage enjoyed by Webb and his habit of
having indiscriminate sex with Gomes and other groupies, the law
recognizes neither of these circumstances as license to demand and
receive any desired sexual act. Like other athletes accused of rape, Webb
failed to comprehend how his actions could be interpreted as criminal.
Barton explained how this situation is particularly conflicting for professional athletes who are accustomed to repeated incidents of casual sex
with multiple partners:

> He wanted to perform other sexual acts that she didn't accept
> or approve of. The law is that women can consent to first base,
> to second base, to third base and say, "That's it. You must
> stop." And the men can't justify it on the basis of arousal or
> anything else.
>
> I'm telling you that a person can have all the consensual
> sex in the world. The law is that if a person doesn't want to

participate in a certain sexual act, they have the right to say "no." (personal interview, 1994)

Webb's disbelief in the rape charges and his subsequent failure to appreciate the potential consequences were reflected in his courtroom demeanor. "He was a very cocky individual through this whole legal proceeding," said Barton. "Number one, he couldn't believe it was happening. Number two, it was all a little bit ridiculous" (personal interview, 1994).

Barton attributed Webb's perception directly to his experiences with groupies in the nightclubs. He stated,

> It was obvious to me that the females at these places throw themselves all over these ball players, so they can't believe that anybody would ever say "no" to them. They're spoiled as men because you got women throwing themselves all over you. After a while, you begin to believe that you personally are something special. (personal interview, 1994)

Lawyers' Strategy

The Obstacles

The pending jury trial to determine the validity of the accuser's allegations against Webb was preceded by considerable media attention. Webb's image was particularly compromised by his well-publicized series of reported violent incidents involving both Gomes and Brown, which resulted in two arrests and a restraining order. In addition, there was the lingering memory that he had falsely accused police officers of a racial act against him in order to avoid the coach's wrath for missing appointments. Finally, there was conclusive medical evidence that indicated the injuries incurred by the complainant were inconsistent with consensual sex. Defense attorney Howard Cooper explained that the jury's perception of Webb was of paramount concern, "You had an inarticulate, not-well-educated, gigantic, black man, who would be accused in front of a Middlesex jury that probably would have been mostly white, of raping a very light-skinned woman" (personal interview, 1994).

The defense adopted a strategy that would ignore the medical evidence, argue that all acts of sex were consensual, and that the witness was a sports groupie who was fictionalizing the story. Cooper explained,

> The medical evidence, as far as we were concerned, was irrelevant to the extent that it showed or tended to prove that a sexual act had taken place. It was by consent. It didn't show and bore no relevance, as far as we were concerned, on whether it was consensual or not. . . . The defense in the case would have been "consent." That anal sex had taken place. (personal interview, 1994)

In an effort to shift the focus from the conduct of Webb, the defense adopted a strategy that would highlight the frequency in which the accuser pursued professional athletes and engaged in consensual sex. They insisted that her criminal allegations were an act of scorn rooted in revenge and designed to exploit Webb's celebrity status. "I question whether this woman ever would have been interested if he wasn't a pro athlete of such high visibility," said Cooper. "Clearly, the media wouldn't have been interested in the case if he wasn't a pro athlete" (personal interview, 1994).

Lawyers for Webb indicated that they intended to present evidence that demonstrated the complainant was a sports groupie who had previous sexual relationships with other professional athletes and that she sought Marcus Webb out for that purpose. "Marcus was prepared to testify that they had quite an extensive sexual relationship that preceded the evening at issue and also was part of the evening at issue," said Cooper. "And that they had done it several times that afternoon and evening" (personal interview).

Gomes's history of involvement with previous Celtics provided the defense with a substantial amount of evidence that would call into question her motive as well as undermine her credibility. Perhaps the most damaging testimony lay in Gomes's reputation for making herself available to athletes. Cooper described the following testimony of a defense witness who was well acquainted with Webb and Gomes:

> He [the witness] warned Webb that she was psycho. I believe the word that he used was that she was a "freak." [It was] a word that I would have assigned to a woman who, [according

to the players interviewed for the case], was just someone who was available—that she liked athletes. (personal interview, 1994)

Depositions were also taken from players, past and present, who were familiar with the complainant and her intimate involvement with other Celtics. "Based upon the testimony that we would have presented at trial from several witnesses, . . . she had had a sexual relationship with Brian Shaw and . . . she had possibly had relationships with other professional athletes," said Cooper (personal interview, 1994). Although the testimony of these players offered little evidence to determine the validity of the accuser's claim on the particular night in question, it greatly influences a jury that is weighing the credibility of the alleged victim.

Another inherent obstacle frequently present in rape cases involving professional athletes is the aggressive pursuit of the accusers by the popular press. The presence of tabloid journalism is used as a tool to attack the alleged victim's motive in filing charges against such a popular man. After Gomes had her name made public by the *Boston Globe,* she was invited to appear on the Sally Jessy Raphael show. The defense was prepared to emphasize this to the jury. "This is a woman who would have taken the witness stand and sat on the Sally Jessy Raphael show," said Cooper (personal interview, 1994).

Victim's Motive

Cooper suggested the following reason for Gomes filing rape charges, undergoing a rape examination, and enduring months of pretrial legal wrangling:

> She subjected herself to this process because she was bitter and wanted to get back at Marcus for leaving her for another woman. I truly believe that this is a case where she truly was scorned. There had been a very short-lived but extremely intense relationship. It had been intensely sexual from the beginning. This was a woman who sent Marcus pretty serious love letters and who was looking to him as someone who she might have a long-term, perhaps permanent, relationship with. It would have been undisputed that Marcus told Ericka

Gomes that he intended to get back together with the mother of his child and that she [Gomes] didn't react well to it. So I believe that that's where this came from. (personal interview, 1994)

The manner in which the defense intended to refute the rape allegations was made clear to the district attorney's office in the aggressive petitioning of the court in pretrial motions. Todd and Cooper solicited the court for permission to admit evidence that would demonstrate Gomes's status as a sports groupie as well as a motive to fabricate the charges against Webb. An intense investigation into the victim's background was begun by first filing a motion to depose former Boston Celtic star Brian Shaw. Even though Shaw was no longer a member of the Celtics and was in no way related to the incident in question, Judge Barton allowed the deposition of Shaw, and it was learned that he had previously had an extensive sexual relationship with Ms. Gomes, a year prior to Webb's arrival in Boston.

Following the judge's ruling to allow deposition of Brian Shaw covering a period of time not to exceed 5 years prior to March 4, 1993, the defense filed a series of motions seeking permission to enter into evidence the contents of the complainant's records of medical and mental health treatment, as well as psychiatric records of the alleged victim going back to childhood. Howard Cooper confirmed that on July 8, the defense attempted to enter into the record evidence of Gomes's bias and motive to lie and a motion to offer proof regarding the sexual activity of Gomes. As Cooper insisted,

This was not a case where you had a guy standing in a dark alley waiting for a stranger. These were two people who had a very intimate relationship. And the jury was going to hear about some very difficult things. Things that you don't typically hear about going on between two people. (personal interview, 1994)

With permission from the court to inform the jury about the frequency of casual sex taking place between not only Webb and Gomes but also between Gomes and other athletes, the jury would be hard pressed not to doubt her credibility. "There were things that would have come out and it would have been terribly ugly," said Cooper. "There was a lot

there that would have put her credibility into very serious question"
(personal interview, 1994).

Disposition

Although it is not unusual for defense lawyers who represent defendants charged with date or acquaintance rape to attempt to establish their
client as something other than a stranger rapist, this tactic is significantly
more persuasive when the accuser has made allegations against a professional athlete with whom she has a history of sexual relations. The
Commonwealth responded by filing a motion to prevent the introduction
of evidence regarding Gomes's alleged sexual activity with individuals
other than Webb. Further, the state attempted to prevent the defense
from introducing evidence of any prior alleged sexual assault complaints
by Gomes. The question of whether to allow Gomes's history of casual
sex with other athletes—particularly Celtics—and her alleged motivation
to lie emerged as the pivotal issues of the case.

Meanwhile, Judge Barton was due to hand down a ruling on the
admissibility of Gomes's psychological, mental, and medical records.
Despite rape shield provisions in the law, the defense was arguing that
these records established her motive to lie. In a meeting held in his
chambers, Barton advised the defense and the district attorney, "Someone
is going to be very unhappy with my ruling [on the admissibility of these
records]" (personal interview, 1994). With this admonition issued just
prior to the start of the weekend, a plea bargain was settled wherein Webb
pleaded guilty to the lesser charge of sexual misconduct in exchange for
a 30-day jail sentence. Prosecutor David Meier concluded,

> The way the case was ultimately disposed had more to do with
> the facts of the case and the victim's background and what,
> in terms of her lifestyle and her relationships with—not only
> other men—but her confidential records of hers which would
> have become presumably public. In terms of her physical
> condition, her mental condition, her emotional background,
> her psychiatric and psychological background, which could
> have created in the jury's mind a real reasonable doubt as to
> what happened.
>
> This was a woman who sought out Marcus Webb, who
> clearly, in everyone's mind, was a sports groupie, who got

involved in a relationship with him, who—at the same time—knew that Marcus Webb was going out with other women, who knew or came to know that he had a child in Alabama, who had sought him out. (personal interview, 1994)

The willful sexual practices of Gomes were a deciding factor. The district attorney's office must consider the prospect of a jury being able and willing to distinguish, as the law does, the difference between consent in prior instances and a single incident of force. Whereas this distinction is never easy, it is particularly challenging when the complainant is a groupie and the accused is a celebrity athlete. Judge Robert Barton summarized,

> The district attorney's office obviously knows they've got weakness in the case because the woman's going to say, "Look, I'm there [Webb's home] voluntarily. I was willing to have sex A, B, C, D, and E, but I just didn't want to do F." And maybe 12 intelligent jurors are going to say, "Hey lady, you put yourself in that position. Who are you with your clothes off after you've done A, B, C, D, and E to say you didn't consent to F? That's your problem. Not guilty." (personal interview, 1994)

Ultimately, her previous acts of consensual sex with the defendant in conjunction with the prospect of other Celtics being called to the witness stand led to the plea arrangement.

> There was a lot on the facts of the case itself which had nothing to do with Marcus Webb whatsoever, which suggested there was a real downside to the likelihood of a conviction. This case was much better from their [the defense] perspective than it was [from] the Commonwealth's. (Meier, personal interview, 1994)

The result is a significantly reduced charge with a punishment that stands in stark contrast to the seriousness of the incident. Although admitting that circumstances surrounding the incident in question greatly hindered the state's ability to prove its case, Judge Barton insisted,

It was a very unusual plea bargain as far as I was concerned. You've taken a fellow who was charged with rape. That's a 20-year felony! He ends up doing a month? Usually most people who are convicted of rape or plead guilty to rape do some serious time. I've been a superior court judge for 16 years and other cases come to my mind. People do serious time. I can't remember a single case where someone has pled guilty to rape and ended up doing a split sentence and ended up with the committed part being 29 or 30 days. You can check far and wide, about the only time we ever see sentences like that is where it's a family thing and the daughter doesn't want to testify against the father. It is very, very rare that anybody gets a suspended sentence for rape or walks away doing 29 days. (personal interview, 1994)

The sexual indulgences that athletes are entitled to can cause jurors to form biased opinions about the defendant because many citizens find such indiscriminate behavior offensive and repugnant. On the day Judge Barton sentenced Webb to serve 30 days in jail, Webb's defense team issued a public statement to the press that read, "Indecent assault and battery is not rape and under no circumstances and in no manner has Mr. Webb pled guilty to anything even approaching rape" (Langner & Gorov, 1993).

Cooper added, "Marcus, even in pleading, maintained his innocence," (personal interview, 1994). Justifying the plea by the fact that Webb was facing a potential 20-year sentence should he be convicted, Cooper reasoned,

The simple realities of it were that a rape conviction carried with it a 20-year potential sentence. A conviction would have meant that he would have no possibility of playing basketball during his twenties as a practical matter. And that type of time, no matter how small the risk, would have ended the opportunity that he had to earn a living.

On the flip side of it was the very attractive prospect that he would not be pleading guilty to rape—that virtually all of his sentence would be suspended. Just by coincidence, Marcus had a contract with an Italian basketball team. In 40 days he had to be there, and I think he felt that this was a way to guarantee that he'd have a life as a professional basketball player.

It really has to do with just the vagaries of the jury system. You never know. And the Commonwealth's offer to him was just a slap on the wrist. Does he carry that label with him as someone convicted of an indecent assault? Absolutely. But there are others in the NBA, even who have rape convictions, who are playing. (personal interview, 1994)

The "Superior Legal Representation" Factor

In the midst of serving his 30-day jail sentence, Webb was permitted to leave prison to stand trial for charges of assault and battery against Quientina Brown. The Commonwealth flew Quientina Brown from Alabama to Boston to testify against Webb. Before a judge, he was convicted and sentenced to a 1-year suspended sentence and 59 days in the house of corrections.

Webb's attorneys planned to appeal the sentence before a six-member jury, but prior to trial, a plea was entered stipulating "no admission of guilt but a finding that there were facts from which he could have been found guilty" (personal interview, 1994). The successful appeal resulted in the 59-day jail sentence being dropped. "There was what could be called a shoving incident involving a slap," said Cooper. "The police were called. They came. She pressed assault and battery charges against him. I believe he should have been acquitted of that charge" (personal interview, 1994).

After completing 28 days of a 30-day sentence for the sexual misconduct conviction, Webb was released from state prison and moved to Europe, where he resumed his professional basketball career. He has flourished there and developed into a premier player.

3

Victoria C. v.
The Cincinnati Bengals

On October 3, 1990, Victoria C. visited a popular nightclub located on the ground floor of a hotel where the Cincinnati Bengals football team was staying. As she stood in the lobby in hopes of meeting a football player, two men wearing Bengals team jackets approached her and asked for directions to the nearest liquor store. She volunteered to drive them. On returning the players to the hotel, she accompanied one of the players to his room for drinks and casual sex.

After having sex, the player, who was a rookie, accompanied Victoria to an adjoining suite where a large group of his teammates were gathered. The player then left the suite and went into an adjoining suite where he propositioned another woman for sex. Meanwhile, Victoria C. was left alone with more than 10 players whom she did not know. The discussion quickly turned to sex and before she could stop what was happening, the players began taking turns penetrating her both vaginally and orally. One by one, they took their clothes off, climbed on the bed, and straddled her.

After approximately 12 players had sexual contact with her, Victoria left the hotel and returned to her home. She did not report to a hospital or to police. Months later, she confided in a psychologist and began receiving counseling from a rape crisis center. Under advice from her counselor, she contacted the Bengals front office 1 year after the incident. Within days, 10 players agreed to pay her $30,000 in exchange for a promise that she would not go public with what had occurred between them.

A "Release of All Claims" was drafted by an attorney representing the players, and she signed and notarized it. In exchange, the attorney wired the $30,000 to her bank account in Washington.

Continuing to suffer major psychological problems, Victoria contacted an attorney and filed a lawsuit seeking damages from the team and the individual players. A jury trial was scheduled to begin in the U.S. District Court at Seattle, but the judge unexpectedly postponed it pending the outcome of a trial to determine the validity of the release Victoria had signed. After hearing the evidence, the jury determined that Victoria's state of mind at the time her signature was affixed to the release was sufficient to deem the contract valid. Although the jurors admitted to believing that a rape had probably taken place, the suit was dismissed by the court due to the validity of the contract.

The Profile

Due to the number of defendants in this case, it would be impractical to describe the background of each individual defendant. Instead, a composite profile has been formed by combining extensive interview data and court documents. Two defendants are referred to throughout this section. I have substituted the name Aaron for defendant #1 and the name Jerome for defendant #2.

Beginning in the section titled "The Incident," the pseudonym "Laura" is used to protect the identity of a witness who was present in the hotel room on the night of the incident between Victoria C. and members of the Cincinnati Bengals.

High School

Aaron grew up in an eastern city, attended public schools, and had both a mother and father in his home. His father was employed as a blue-collar laborer while his mother remained unemployed throughout his childhood. Although his parents expected him to complete high school and hoped he would attend college, neither parent had any formal education. "My mother or dad didn't graduate from high school," he explained (personal interview, 1994).

As a high school student, Aaron's time away from the classroom was primarily spent playing sports. He participated in virtually no other extracurricular activities. Other than the ball field, his surroundings encouraged him to avoid situations that would land him in trouble. "We didn't have a lot of activities such as the other schools," he said. "You kind of went home and kind of stayed out of trouble" (personal interview, 1994). Although many of his peers had little opportunity to escape this cycle, his excellence in sports distinguished him from his classmates and suggested a way out of this environment. "Athletics was what brought the attention [to me] of course," he said. "I was pretty much kind of an area hero" (personal interview, 1994).

The adulation that he received for physical exploits made him a celebrity within his own school. Despite his excellence in athletics, his school seldom attracted local media. The newspapers were more inclined to cover suburban schools, thus Aaron did not receive notoriety outside of his neighborhood. "Being the background I'm from [sic] and the school I went to, I never had an article written in the paper about me," he stated. "A lot of people had never heard of me until I went to the University" (personal interview, 1994).

Although the press gave him little attention, college recruiters discovered his exceptional abilities and began pursuing him during his junior year of high school. Not only did recruiting make Aaron the subject of unprecedented attention, but it also exposed him to a lifestyle that he had never before experienced. Going into his senior year of high school, Aaron had never traveled outside his home city. He explained,

> Recruiting was first, letters my junior year. Then, my senior year, more letters—tons of them. For me recruiting was special because it was getting notoriety from kind of the pits, the bottom of the barrel so to speak. You get wined and dined. You got a nice meal. You got to see these great facilities. You stayed in the Grand Hyatt. That was the glitz and the glamour of it. I was offered a scholarship pretty much any place I wanted to go. (personal interview, 1994)

As a prized athlete, coaches were flying to his home from across the country and in turn they were flying him to their respective campuses to view the facilities. There were few players with Aaron's potential, thus a bidding war was entered into by recruiting coaches. The nature of this system forced nationally famous coaches—some of whose incomes exceeded a quarter of a million dollars annually, to cater to and bestow a tremendous amount of adulation on 17-year-old Aaron, who lived in a home where money was not plentiful. Prohibited from offering financial incentives, coaches impressed Aaron in other ways that appeal to young adolescents with aspirations to become professional athletes. "There's a wide range of things that attract different players, . . . material things, gettin' paid or a car or something of that nature," said Aaron. "But when you get to meet the person that was in the NFL or headed to the NFL or was really notable, that was the special part of it" (personal interview, 1994).

College

The number of black teenagers being offered college scholarships to play football and basketball has been steadily rising over the past decade. For the 1993-1994 school year, the NCAA reported that blacks comprised just 9% of the undergraduate enrollment at over 300 Division I institutions. Yet 65% of the male basketball players and 50% of the football players at those same schools were black (*1994 NCAA Division,* 1994). This significant discrepancy is largely due to universities expressing more interest in black athletes than in prospective black students. Increasingly, recruiters from prestigious universities retrieve players from economically depressed neighborhoods to come and display their physical talents for 4 years in exchange for a scholarship. As Aaron explained,

> There are so many black players. We know the black outweigh the white and we know where the vast majority come from. So it's kind of like a second-degree slavery. Coaches go into the inner city. They grab out of there and they say, "You generate this money for me for four years," and then they spit you out of the system. (personal interview, 1994)

After committing to attend a major university for the purpose of playing football, Aaron left his home and headed for a rural campus. He was cognizant on his arrival that the only reason he was attending such a prestigious institution was because of his athletic abilities. This fact was emphasized during his first football game. He looked up to see 95,000 fans in the stadium, without a black face in sight. "I always thought I was the majority instead of the minority because I was raised in a predominantly black neighborhood," he said. "Everybody, including me, knows that your education revolves around your athletic ability" (personal interview, 1994).

Although feeling inferior as a student, athletes find their arrival on campus is accompanied by instant recognition and adulation by the student body. Becoming the subject of fan support suffocates the disproportionate academic standing between some athletes and their school peers. Rather than focus on the disparity between them and the other students, athletes easily become content to revel in their newfound fame. "It felt great because you stuck out," Aaron recalled, referring to his impressions as a freshman. "It felt special simply because you were recognized. I had never been recognized before. Outside of my neighborhood nobody knew who I was" (personal interview, 1994).

Along with the instant respect that was afforded Aaron because of his physical skills, he became the recipient of privileges that fortified his impression that he was not an ordinary college student. He described the following:

> You had certain things that wasn't [sic] accessible to other people. For example, when you want to change your class, you didn't have to go stand in that long line. You went over to a certain person and they changed it for you. We didn't have to eat the hospital food the other dormitories ate. We had our own special cafeteria. At that time, we had an athletic dorm—so everything we got was special. We got the first class. We got the tennis shoes. You get your brand new Nikes and, of course, we all walked around in them. You got your sweats. Little things like that mean so much because you come from virtually nothing and then all of a sudden you get here.
>
> You have all the alumni while your playing. There was a lot of advantages. I couldn't see a negative one. It was a fun time because all the special attention you got . . . was just solely based on being an athlete. (personal interview, 1994)

It is the suddenness and abundance of special treatment that instills in the student-athlete a sense of elitism. Aaron's ego was constantly stroked by coaches, alumni, and cheering students. This reinforced the lessons of high school that taught that excelling in sports brings off-the-field benefits. Aaron recalled,

> *Being notarized [sic] was special for me simply because I never had the attention. Your self-esteem level kinda rises. And that's when the ego builds and the confidence builds. And I think that's why an athlete has that prowess, that "I can take on the world." And that's where it comes from. Because when you get to college, people notice you and say all these good things about you. (personal interview, 1994)*

Four years of playing college football further reinforced Aaron's perception of invincibility. Players of his caliber realize early that a professional contract awaits them and it is only a matter of time before they will be the recipients of abundant wealth. The necessity of a college degree is arbitrarily discarded because it is of no importance in obtaining a professional career in sports. Like many professional athletes, Aaron completed his 4 years of eligibility and was drafted out of college without graduating.

The Professional

The wealth obtained by Aaron, immediately after leaving college to sign a professional contract with the Cincinnati Bengals, vaulted him past the income level of nearly all college-educated, working adults in America. "My sister-in-law is an engineer," he adeptly pointed out. "For every year I play, it would take her twenty years to make the salary that I make—and she's an engineer" (personal interview, 1994).

He was now a superstar of national exposure. His newly acquired wealth brought a new form of power. The power to appeal to so many people is just one of the many things that distinguishes professional athletes from other individuals who may be in a position of power. He explained,

> I've always noticed one thing about being an athlete as opposed to being a politician or a millionaire. The difference is that with being an athlete you get notoriety, wealth, and power. If you go out to start a business or if you are very

successful in business, more than likely you just have wealth.
You won't have notoriety. And then you see them guys turn
to politicians to get that notoriety and power whereas athletes
seem to have that power—that control. (personal interview,
1994)

The Access

The scenario of young, attractive ladies pursuing professional football players in hip clubs and bars reinforces the players' sense of power
and superiority. On becoming a member of the Cincinnati Bengals, Aaron
became one of an elite group of men who shared a very uncommon
lifestyle. One teammate, Jerome—who later was named as a defendant
in the rape case, allowed the access and involvement with women to
become a vice. Using his superior position as a professional football
player, Jerome exploited the unlimited opportunities to meet and have
sex with women. Constantly frequenting popular nightclubs, he received
the adulation of countless women who were willing to participate in
sexual relationships with him in exchange for his association. A steady
indulgence in this behavior produced an insatiable appetite to have
women and control them. Aaron explained,

> Jerome was spoiled, always a high glitz, high glamour type
> person. He had a Mercedes, top of the line. And he drove a
> Lamborghini. He walked around with a grand in his pocket.
> I mean he had wealth. He had this very plush, gorgeous home.
> When he got girls, he wanted his way. He wanted to control
> them, their bodies, everything. He was a spoiled brat. (per-
> sonal interview, 1994)

Attorney Spencer Hall, who was subsequently retained to represent
a group of Bengals players accused of rape, explained the connection
between women and the fame afforded athletes:

> They [athletes] are people who are famous. They are people
> with money. They are no different than rock stars, movie stars
> in that they have more opportunity. . . . I think a lot of them
> are pretty inexperienced, unsophisticated people presented

with opportunities that a lot of the rest of society aren't presented with. (personal interview, 1994)

Attorney Brad Keller, who was also retained as defense counsel and represented a separate group of accused Bengals, suggested that the ready availability of certain women to professional athletes impacts the way players view all women. Although there are very few women who have interest in sexual relationships with professional athletes, it is this peculiar group of women with whom some athletes regularly surround themselves. "Women chase them," said Keller. "If you are a healthy, red-blooded, American male you don't have the access that pros do. I think it impacts their views on the sexes" (personal interview, 1994).

Aaron indicated that the confidence required to survive in the profession of football, when coupled with the willingness of women— particularly fashionable, white women—creates an atmosphere for women to be taken advantage of and used at the player's discretion. "I think that had a lot to do with confidence . . . probably an ego thing," he said. "White women are easy to pick up. They are easy to manipulate. They are just easy to get the things you want out of them" (personal interview, 1994).

Relationships in which consensual sex is the primary purpose come with ease to professional athletes who are so inclined. Players who enjoy this access become conditioned to brief encounters with sex partners and then discarding these women with little afterthought. Spencer Hall explained that the degree of fame achieved by the Bengals players furnished them with opportunities for behavior that is difficult for much of society to understand:

I do think one factor is that, to the extent that you have behavior that you view as risquéé [or] immoral, I would think there's more opportunity presented to certainly famous athletes than to a lot of the rest of society. That if there was more [sexual] activity, that may be why. (personal interview, 1994)

The Incident

For a 1-week period during October 1990, the Cincinnati Bengals football team stayed at the Double Tree Inn located outside Seattle. Hotel employees indicated that a steady stream of women frequented the Bengals' floor throughout their stay. Hotel security added that they had more problems with security during the Bengals stay than at any other time, particularly with players' attempts to tape over latches and locks in an attempt to violate team curfew rules without getting caught.

Midway through the week, the hotel lounge held its weekly "Ladies Night." Hoping to meet a player, Victoria C. positioned herself in the hotel lobby. Players Lynn James and Solomon Wilcots approached her and requested directions to a liquor store. Victoria had attended the game between the Bengals and the Seahawks 2 days prior and immediately recognized that these two men were players. As a result, she offered to escort them to buy liquor and return them to the hotel. On arriving back at the hotel, Solomon Wilcots went his own way, while Lynn James invited Victoria to his room for a drink.

When James and Victoria entered his room, they found James's roommate, Reggie Rembert, and a female companion, Laura, occupying the bedroom area of the suite. Laura described the following events:

> Reggie and I were sitting on the beds in the back watching TV. And then Lynn came in with the girl [Victoria]. She was pretty full of herself. She was dressed in tight clothing. She had on tight leggings and pumps and a shirt that kind of showed her stomach a little bit. She was primping. She basically knew what she was up there for—to go back and have sex with Lynn. (personal interview, 1994)

Rembert and Laura moved to another room in the suite, while James and Victoria C. had a drink and proceeded to engage in consensual sexual intercourse. After willfully engaging in sex, both Victoria and Lynn left the bedroom area and entered the adjoining suite occupied by the team's most celebrated player, Ickey Woods. Within the room, a group of players were gathered. It soon became clear to all present that Victoria had just participated in sex with James. The players and Victoria soon engaged in a flirtatious and crude conversation of a sexual nature. Before long, some of the players had removed their pants and likewise, Victoria C. was undressed. Woods later confirmed that her actions and statements convinced them that she wanted to have sex with the group of them.

The players' capacity to indulge in a degree of sexual activity that seems excessive is evidenced by the actions of roommates James and

Rembert. While Victoria was in Woods's room with a group of other teammates, Rembert temporarily left his date, Laura, in his suite and entered Woods's room. Concurrently, James, who had just completed intercourse with Victoria, entered the room where Laura was and proceeded to initiate sex with her. She described the events as follows:

> Lynn James came in and he went back into the bed area. He motioned for me to "Come here, come here."
>
> And I'm like looking at him and saying, "What do you want?"
>
> And he's like, "Come here."
>
> So I walked back to the bedroom where he was and he started putting his hands on my waist and stuff. I guess he was just assuming that since I was up in the room that I was up there for sex. (personal interview, 1994)

Meanwhile, Rembert, who was spending the evening with Laura, proceeded to penetrate Victoria in the presence of his teammates in Woods's room. After returning to his suite where Laura was waiting, the following discussion took place:

> Reggie came back out and he's like, "You know, you wouldn't believe what's going on over there."
>
> And I said, "What?"
>
> And he said, "She's just over there having sex with everybody."
>
> And Reggie wasn't concerned or anything like that. It was just kind of a matter-of-fact statement that she was having sex with 'em. (personal interview, 1994)

World-famous millionaire athletes were standing around eating food and drinking beverages while watching each other participating in serial acts of vaginal and oral intercourse, yet it was perceived by the players as a matter-of-fact event. Woods explained, "I walked in [to my room] and she [Victoria] was having intercourse with a couple of guys. She gave a couple of guys some oral sex. . . . And when that happens, they [the football players] consider that [Victoria] a freak" ("The Rules of," 1993).

Although it is indisputable that Victoria willfully participated in casual sex with Lynn James, and it is plausible that her actions and dialogue indicated a desire for further sexual contact with perhaps another player, the episode swiftly escalated out of control. "And that's when all the other guys bombarded the room and I didn't know what was going on," said James. "I can't control those other guys' actions . . . and I did not, um . . . in no form or fashion . . . try to bring that upon [Victoria C.]" (phone machine transcript, May 11, 1992).

A succession of players, ranging in weight from 185 lbs to nearly 300 lbs each, took turns penetrating Victoria who, according to her attorney, was "naked on her hands and knees" (personal interview, 1994). In addition to being drowned out in the noise and excitement, the concept of consent, which presupposes that a woman possesses power equivalent to that of her male counterpart, was negated with Victoria being surrounded by a group of large men whose manhood was at stake. One of the defendants admitted that, "She said 'No'," but only after events were far beyond her ability to control. Further, he added,

> There was a lot of noise, music. . . . It was like, "Hey [name deleted], your turn buddy." Well, it was very hard for you to say, "Nah. No. No," because you're gonna get ragged about it. You're gonna get teased about it. (personal interview, 1994)

An estimated 2 hours after initially entering the hotel, Victoria C. exited to her car and drove directly to her home. She did not go to a hospital, nor did she report the incident to hotel security or the police. She visited a rape crisis center months later and began receiving therapy. Only after a rape counselor convinced her to be tested for the AIDS virus did Victoria finally confess to her doctor that she had been raped. During this time, her behavior was quite erratic. Her 14-year-old son later testified, "She was crying all the time, doing strange things. She turned on all the lights at night. She stayed up late, take showers all the time. And she washed things all the time—caps, shoes, clothes" (Farrey, 1993a).

After nearly 8 months of treatment and counseling, Victoria's rape crisis counselor advised her to contact the Bengals front office and notify them of the incident and seek a formal apology from the team. Receiving notification 12 months after the incident took place, Bengals' team counsel, Mike Brown, alerted the only two players whom Victoria had identified by name—Ickey Woods and Tim McGee—of the allegations being made against them. Both players were made aware of the potential implications of the accusation against them and were provided with the name and telephone number of prominent Cincinnati criminal defense attorney, James Perry.

Woods immediately engaged in a series of phone conversations with Victoria and initiated attempts to prevent the allegations from becoming public knowledge. Victoria's initial call to the team office was fielded by Al Heim, public-relations director for the Bengals. He would later testify at trial that Victoria "made no mention of money when she called" (Farrey, 1993b). Nonetheless, Woods, after making contact with attorney James Perry, orchestrated a payoff scheme. Functioning as spokesperson for the other players involved, he offered Victoria $30,000 in exchange for her silence.

Perry drafted a formal "Release of All Claims," which stipulated that the players contributing to the payment "wish to remain anonymous and further desire that the terms of the settlement receive no public disclosure" (*Victoria C. v. Cincinnati Bengals,* Defendants' Trial Brief, 1992). In exchange for the preserved identity of players and a notarized promise to not make her claims public, Victoria would be paid $30,000. Perry's contract was faxed to Victoria in Spokane, Washington, where she signed it, took it to a used-car dealership to be notarized, and returned it via Express Mail to Perry's Cincinnati office. Perry then wired the players' money to Victoria's bank account in Washington (*Victoria C. v. Cincinnati Bengals,* Defendant's Trial Brief, 1992, pp. 6-7).

One of the key players accused, Tim McGee, did not contribute to the payoff, maintaining his innocence from the moment he became aware of the alleged incident. He referred to the payoff "as an admission of guilt" (personal interview, 1994). On the other hand, Woods, who admitted that a considerable amount of sexual contact had taken place with the accuser, insisted that reaching a financial settlement was simply a matter of convenience. "Most professional athletes don't want to go through the whole bit of trying to prove that they're innocent," he said ("The Rules of," 1993)

The Court's Response

Jurisdiction

The players' admission of sexual intercourse coupled with a denial of rape conflicted with the professional advice Victoria was receiving in response to her medical condition. Thus, she ultimately decided to go ahead and seek damages from the players. Less than 6 months after receiving the $30,000 payoff, she filed suit against the team and individual players. In her complaint, she alleged that she was

> brutally and sadistically raped, orally and vaginally, over two hours by thirteen to fifteen Bengal players who were two to three times her size on the "team floor." . . . [I]ndividual player defendants intentionally, unlawfully, violently, and without plaintiff's consent, indeed, despite her pleas for help and mercy, assaulted and battered plaintiff by forcibly committing repeated acts of carnal intercourse and physical abuse upon plaintiff. (*Victoria C. v. Cincinnati Bengals,* Second Amended Complaint, 1992, p. 6)

The Assembly of Lawyers

Victoria's suit initially identified 19 players as having either participated in or witnessed the incident. The sensational charges triggered a legal defense machine rarely seen in rape cases. Because Victoria identified the Bengals franchise, as well as the individual players, as separate defendants, the team retained its own lawyers to represent the organization. Meanwhile, the players left much of their defense planning up to their individual agents, who represent them in contract negotiations and other noncriminal legal matters. The player agents arranged for top law firms from Seattle and Cincinnati to gather for a series of interviews to be conducted by the agents. From those interviews, two teams of lawyers were assembled: one to represent players who admitted being present in the hotel room on the night in question, and a second team to act as counsel for players who claimed they were not present in the room on the night of the alleged incident.

Neither of the two Seattle firms retained to act as defense counsel had particular experience representing defendants accused of sexual violence. Rather, Byrnes & Keller are among the city's finest trial lawyers known for defending white-collar crime, whereas Spencer Hall of Mundt, MacGregor, Happel, Falconer, Zulauf & Hall claimed he was experienced in "a broad range of business work and civil litigation" (personal interview, 1994). Judge Walter T. McGovern, who took over the case after the first judge recused himself, insisted that the Bengals players "couldn't have had better representation. Those lawyers were very good" (personal interview, 1994). His law clerk, Phil Lucid, concurred, "The Bengals' attorneys were very very skilled. The defense attorneys really did a number on her" (personal interview, 1994). This assessment comes from a judge and clerk whose careers span over 20 years in the courts, and who have been assigned very high-profile political corruption cases, including the famous Neo-Nazi trial, as well as antitrust and securities fraud cases.

The Athletes' Perception of the Incident

After learning that they were the subject of a lawsuit involving multiple counts of rape, the players who were present on the night of the incident in question defended their actions as an incident of consensual sex participated in by a small group of players.

Although there was bilateral agreement between the accused players that a rape did not occur, one defendant offered the following explanation after judgment had been rendered:

> One bad thing about us, we've learned to accept challenges. We've grown to accept the challenge of an opponent, so to speak. We, as athletes, have always accepted challenges—"I can beat you. I can physically beat you. I can mentally beat you." If we feel for one split second that I cannot achieve or I cannot beat the opponent, mentally we have failed.
>
> I think the challenge here was not even with the young lady. The challenge here might have been with the other guys. I think it was basically teenage peer pressure. It's peer pressure. It's the pressure to meet this challenge around the quote unquote "guys." The peer pressure to perform in front of the guys like the pressure to drink in front of the guys.
>
> For example, a married man normally would have just slid on out that room, but players get caught up in it. And that's peer pressure. It may be peer pressure for 30-year-old kids, but it's pretty much in the same line with a teenager who's been asked to drink a shot of vodka. Do you want that label? Do you want the ramifications that come with saying "no"? (personal interview, 1994)

The Bengals players demonstrated a complete inability to appreciate the gravity of their actions. There was consensus among those involved that what had occurred was morally acceptable, and certainly not criminal. One defendant said,

> The question I would ask is "When are we allowed to be humans?" Are we allowed private moments? If I'm some type of sexual freak that love [sic] five women could I do that in my time at home? Is there a right to do it? Just because you're an athlete, that doesn't separate you from the other desires, needs, fantasies, etc., etc. You can't say that athletes don't pick up *Playboy* magazines. It's not fair to always make us the role model.
>
> What I mean by that is that a single guy doesn't have the pleasure or doesn't have the same ability that a married guy has. A married guy can go in the privacy of his home and whatever happens happens. And that's fine because you're married and that's morally right. But a single guy gotta [sic] get it from somewhere. (personal interview, 1994)

His emphasis is on the player's need—his need to "get it from somewhere." Women who consent to be alone with professional athletes have no input as to what "it" consists of. Victoria's presence in the players' bedroom suggests that she yielded to any acts that players felt inclined to commit. The repetition of women participating in this form of sexual relationship without ever voicing dissatisfaction makes it increasingly difficult for players to comprehend that their actions may be defined as criminal. "Even the warrior drops his guards at some time," one of the defendants said in reference to the incident. "Even the warrior has a weakness. It was a human act. It [the incident in the hotel room] wasn't brutality. It was in fun, enjoyment, not as in brutality or something that could be classified as even criminal" (personal interview, 1994).

Immediately after Victoria brought rape charges against them, the players insisted that money was her motive. Team members argued that the charges were merely a fame-seeking ploy to exploit their celebrity status. After labeling Victoria a freak, Woods subsequently defined freak as "a woman [sic] who have sex with a number of guys" ("The Rules of," 1993). He went on to add, "[A] woman out trying to get some money from some ballplayers. She was in dire need of some money. Her medical bills were piling up on her, so she came up with, 'Hey, I'll go with these [players]—I'll go to these professional players and blackmail them into giving me some money'" ("The Rules of," 1993).

The Lawyers' Strategy

The Obstacles

The lawyers put forth the players' rather crude account in a legal and less offensive tone. They treated it as a contract issue in which she had received payment. Thus, the players were not liable for additional damages. Their strategy was to convince a jury that Victoria C. willingly participated in multiple forms of intercourse with numerous players in succession. "The biggest obstacle for the defense was getting people to accept that a woman would engage in multiple, serial sexual encounters," said defense counsel Brad Keller (personal interview, 1994).

The problem is that a jury of everyday citizens is completely unaccustomed to the sexual ways of professional athletes. Defense counsel Spencer Hall concurred that the overriding challenge was

> the ability of you or anyone else to conceive of this kind of sexual activity occurring. That, obviously, was a concern of mine in thinking about trying this case to a jury. In other words, would the average juror believe that a woman, or anyone, is capable of going into a room with a bunch of strangers and voluntarily engaging in this kind of sexual activity? (personal interview, 1994)

Jurors are asked to view the evidence presented to them and apply the law as it is explained in jury instructions distributed by the judge. Citizens inevitably bring their individual moral standards and value judgments into the jury box. In the absence of witnesses, jurors' individual biases become paramount. Because the lifestyles of professional football players and female groupies are so terribly uncommon, jurors simply fail to conceive of the experiences of either litigant. Spencer Hall explained,

> I think it is real easy to bring your own moral standards to these kinds of situations and make judgments that are dif-

ferent than the judgments that need to be made in the case to decide it one way or the other. This was not a case about whether it was good judgment for a football player to have sex with a strange woman who he didn't know—even one-on-one. It wasn't a case about whether it is good judgment or good morals to have group sex.

In terms of this case . . . people's judgments and whether having sex in front of another person is right or wrong or embarrassing were all things that concerned us in terms of how a jury might react. (personal interview, 1994)

Shifting the emphasis away from the conduct of the defendants and onto the accuser, defense attorneys described Victoria as a groupie who pursued these players. Further, they emphasized that she pursued them for the purpose of sex and, in fact, aggressively initiated the sexual activity. Finally, they suggested that her rape allegations were motivated by a quest for money and fame—pointing out that the charges conveniently corresponded with the Mike Tyson case. "Victoria C. was attracted to these people because they were celebrities, because they were football players," said Spencer Hall (personal interview, 1994).

Victim's Motive

While portraying Victoria as a groupie who pursued these players purely for sex, defense lawyers used the athletes' million-dollar salaries and national recognition as a means to further remove them from responsibility for their actions. They suggested that the players' status was being exploited. Spencer Hall argued,

She wanted to try and get money. So she went and shouted her story from the rooftops—figuratively speaking. In terms of conjuring up horrors and so forth, I think that's the game that Victoria C. was playing. So I always was concerned that the jury would hear those accusations. It would be hard for them to be objective because their minds would run wild. (personal interview, 1994)

Whereas their fame and money were what granted them access and license to voluminous sexual encounters, that same status was being employed to insulate them from accountability before a jury. According to the defense, the women who willfully sought out these Bengals players were fully responsible for whatever took place in the players' hotel rooms. In other words, the women assumed the risk. "The plaintiff was an opportunist who was fabricating the incident for monetary gain and a desire to thrust herself into the public limelight," said Keller. "It is more than coincidence that she did this when the Mike Tyson case was in the news" (personal interview, 1994).

In preparation for trial, the defense petitioned the court through briefs and memos designed to weaken the complainant's credibility and portray her as a groupie who was the initiator of the sexual incidents in question. The following is an excerpt from a pretrial brief filed under seal:

> In the face of these allegations [that a 98-lb woman was brutally raped by a group of football players who were two to three times her size], it would be inadequate to simply tell the jury these defendants deny these allegations and that defendants contend that any sexual contact that took place was consensual.
>
> The likely reaction of the jury, lacking further information, would be extreme skepticism about defendant's position. (*Victoria C. v. Cincinnati Bengals,* Trial Brief of Defendants, 1993, p. 3)

The brief went on to lay out the players' description of what took place:

1. Plaintiff stripped off her clothes in the presence of some of the players.
2. Plaintiff walked into the bedroom where the incident occurred on her own and placed herself nude on the bed.
3. Sitting nude on the bed, plaintiff pulled down the sweat pants of one player, took his penis, and placed it in her mouth.
4. After plaintiff initiated sex with one or more of the players, she took time out to drink some beer and later go to the toilet.
5. Plaintiff sought extensive sexual contact with the players. She took the penises of numerous players and placed them in her mouth.

6. On her own, plaintiff went into the bathroom and hid during bed check so that she could stay until later in the evening. When the coach came in for bed check, she made no effort to ask for help. To the contrary, she stayed hidden so that she could continue her activities. (*Victoria C. v. Cincinnati Bengals,* Trial Brief of Defendants, 1993, p. 4)

This crude portrayal of the accuser casts her in a most disparaging light while suggesting that the players merely accommodated her animalistic appetites. Elsewhere in the brief, they described the complainant as the aggressor and informed the court that this account was corroborated by a witness:

The defendants who were present testified that Plaintiff complained that her clothes did not fit properly, undressed before a group of players, requested that they have sex with her, and then engaged several players in various acts including intercourse. Defendants' contentions are corroborated by a witness, [name deleted], who saw Plaintiff after the encounter with James and contradicts Plaintiff's account in several crucial respects. (*Victoria C. v. Cincinnati Bengals,* Trial Brief of Defendants, 1993, p. 4)

In addition to portraying the alleged victim as the aggressor, pretrial briefs were used to discredit the complainant by offering evidence to support the notion that she was merely trying to extort money from these wealthy athletes. According to the defendants' trial brief, "Plaintiff used the money to buy a sports car, lease an expensive house complete with swimming pool, and pay off a debt owed to her boyfriend's grandparents. She spent none of it on medical or mental health care" (*Victoria C. v. Cincinnati Bengals,* Trial Brief of Defendants, 1993, p. 7).

Disposition

One of the defense's arguments to refute the credibility of Victoria's claim was the fact that she failed to press criminal charges against the players. Her background was a deterrent to reporting the incident to police. She had a history of interest in professional athletes. Furthermore, she had engaged in consensual sex on the night in question after willfully going to the hotel room of the players. These factors would be extremely discouraging to a district attorney and suspicious to a jury. "When you look at her particular history, she does seem to have an attraction to sports people or people who play sports," insisted Victoria Vreeland, co-counsel for Victoria C. "She has a history of dating sports people who are fairly celebrated" (personal interview, 1994). Vreeland went on to state the following:

> Consent is their defense, so they're going to say, "She likes football players. She hung around them in the past. She was there voluntarily. She went up to their room voluntarily. She had voluntary sex with Lynn James." And to all that we say, "You're right. You're right. You're right. You're right." (personal interview, 1994)

Vreeland further pointed out that Victoria's presence at the Seahawks training camp, as well as her possession of various professional players' autographs, only substantiated the impression that she was a groupie. The state had to consider these factors before taking on a criminal case that required the jury to render a verdict of guilty only if they were convinced beyond a reasonable doubt. Vreeland insisted,

> This state nor any state would not have prosecuted because there was insufficient evidence to prove guilt beyond a reasonable doubt. They [the district attorney's office] wouldn't pursue it because there was no way they could possibly win—because of the burden of proof.
> There's a lot of debate with lawyers, whether you want to go civil or criminal first, because the criminal case takes precedence in the courts and it goes faster than a civil case and because the burden is higher. They [the players] could be found "not guilty" criminally but still be found civilly responsible. (personal interview, 1994)

Although the burden of proof is notably less in civil cases (a preponderance of evidence is required, as opposed to beyond a reasonable doubt), Victoria's lawyers were still unable to persuade the jury. After the original trial date had been scheduled, Judge McGovern delayed the rape trial, opting to first hold a trial to determine the validity of the agreement entered into by the players and Victoria. He explained,

> If the release was valid, then I didn't have to get into the sordid claims or counterclaims—whatever they may be. I did not want to go into all of the—what I heard were—the sordid details.
>
> I didn't make a decision one way or the other as to what occurred. I knew there were several cases of relationship there between some professional football players and the plaintiff. But to what extent it was consensual and to what extent it was not consensual I don't know. And I simply did not have to make that decision. (personal interview, 1994)

Judge Coughenour, the original judge assigned to the case, had denied the defendants' request to limit discovery to material relevant to the validity of the release, and ruled that the matter of the alleged rape should be argued before a jury (*Victoria C. v. Cincinnati Bengals*, Order No. C92-658M, 1993). Shortly after the case was reassigned to Judge McGovern, he moved to bifurcate due to the existing "Release of All Claims," which stipulated that the plaintiff was barred from suing the players. McGovern was clearly within his jurisdiction to bifurcate, but his disapproving view of the defendants' alleged behavior suggests a motive for trying the validity of the document prior to trying the validity of the rape claim. He stated the following:

> Well maybe I am naive, but I don't know how anybody can engage in group sex. Just your relationship of what occurred there was sort of nauseating.
>
> I'm not sure I ever heard them [the players] say that they were doing it in front of each other. Maybe the implication was there and I was trying to hide my eyes, ears, and nose to it because it is not very pleasant. Frankly, I don't remember that. But it wouldn't surprise me if that's what they were saying. I cannot conceive how people can do that. (personal interview, 1994)

The players openly and unequivocally stated that they had engaged in a consensual sexual encounter with the complainant and that numerous players took turns penetrating the victim. The issue did not rest on whether or not multiple acts of intercourse took place, but rather on whether it was the result of force or consent. The sheer outrageousness of the players' actions with Victoria served as further insulation from accountability for the players. Their own account of what took place, which is not considered criminal, is so far removed from human decency that the judge had no interest in hearing the allegations unless it was absolutely necessary. On reflection, Judge McGovern questioned,

> I guess there is such a thing as group sex. And then you wonder, how do they get caught up in it? Do they get caught up in it only because they happened to be in an atmosphere at the particular time which is conducive to "Let's let everything go"? But there are people who are smart enough, morally correct enough to get up and walk out. Some, less so, are maybe talked into it by their fellow peers—their football friends. (personal interview, 1994)

The jury was convened and heard testimony on the validity of the document and the alleged victim's state of mind at the time she signed the release. After hearing from three accused players, the victim, various medical personnel, and other witnesses, the jury found in favor of the players. With a ruling that the release was valid, Victoria was legally prevented from seeking damages against the players.

The "Superior Legal Representation" Factor

Particularly in cases where there are virtually no witnesses and no physical evidence, outcomes are determined largely by the lawyers' success or failure at portraying a defendant as more believable than the accuser. The resources of professional players put them at a profound advantage. It allows accused rapists to employ legal experts who are exceptional lawyers. They subject alleged victims to extreme scrutiny. Because the backgrounds of most women who willfully sleep with athletes are checkered, the lawyers are provided with a wealth of background evidence that prejudices the jury in a most detrimental way.

Although the athletes involved in these rape cases have equally checkered backgrounds, this information is not presented as evidence because it lacks probative value. The complaining witness, on the other hand, is subject to character scrutiny, as deft defense lawyers insist that it determines the validity of her claim. The lawyers representing the Cincinnati Bengals successfully steered the focus to Victoria C.'s history and thus ensured a favorable decision for the players in the civil case. Judge McGovern's law clerk, Phil Lucid, who was required to watch 36 hours of videotaped deposition of Victoria C. detailing the alleged rape, was deeply disturbed by the allegations. "I didn't look back convinced that she was not seriously violated by some of those people," he said (personal interview, 1994). In terms of why she became less appealing to the jury and why she had her credibility compromised, it clearly rested in the lawyers' successful portrayal of the complainant as responsible for the incident. Lucid explained,

> I found her to be far less convincing in court. The defense attorneys asked very particularized questions. I mean she was just reduced to almost groveling. I just gradually became concerned about whether or not she didn't have some responsibility for being there. She didn't come out of it looking as though I'm sure she would have wanted to look before a jury. (personal interview, 1994)

The questions, "Why was she there?" and "Isn't she responsible for what took place?" present more challenges to a jury when the defendant or defendants are well-known professional football players. The answers to these questions revealed a woman with some attraction to professional athletes. It lends support to the players' claim that she consented to be with them. The ability to present this message is enough to raise a sufficient doubt in jurors' minds.

4

Indiana v. Michael G. Tyson

Black Expo 1991 invited Mike Tyson to Indianapolis in hopes of generating publicity for their week-long festivities, particularly the beauty pageant. It was just another stop on the heavyweight champion's whirlwind schedule of appearances that occupied his time between training and fights. Onlookers stared and applauded as Tyson flirted and touched each swimsuit-clad contestant. During his brief pose with Rhode Island's 18-year-old Desiree Washington, Tyson suggested that she accompany him to some celebrity parties later that evening. Overwhelmed and flattered by personal attention from one of the most recognizable black men in America, Washington indicated that she was interested.

Later that evening, Tyson attended rap artist B Angie B's concert at the Hoosier Dome. During the show he remained backstage, surrounded by countless women. Following the performance, he and a small entourage went to some of the finer clubs in Indianapolis, where Tyson ordered extravagant wines that were left unopened and unpaid for. Finally, at 1:30 a.m., Tyson's limousine pulled up in front of the hotel where Washington was staying.

After two telephone calls from Tyson via his cellular phone, Washington had still not agreed to come down to meet him. She was in pajamas, her makeup removed, and her hair no longer done up. But her roommates suggested she reconsider. They reminded her that this was a once-in-a-lifetime opportunity. In a rush, she dressed and joined Tyson in his limousine. Before going to any parties, Tyson suggested a brief stop at his hotel to pick up a few things and an additional bodyguard. Star-struck, Washington accepted his offer to see the luxurious private suite.

Once inside, Tyson turned on the television and began asking questions about Washington's background. Within minutes the conversation became sprinkled with sexual innuendo. After he sat down and placed his hand on her, Washington became nervous and retreated to the bathroom. When she exited the bathroom, Tyson was virtually naked. In her effort to flee the room, she was grabbed, stripped and pinned down on the bed. "Don't fight me," he said as she begged him to stop. "You can't win. Don't fight me. Just relax" (Garrison & Roberts, 1994, p. 27).

He proceeded to force her legs apart while holding her arms, lubricate her with his tongue, and forcibly penetrate her. Not wearing a condom, he withdrew just prior to ejaculation.

Later the following morning, she entered Methodist Hospital and underwent an examination, and gave a statement to the sex-crimes unit police officer. After 2 days of consideration, she decided to press charges against Tyson. Eventually, both Washington and Tyson testified before a grand jury, which found probable cause and issued an indictment charging Tyson with first-degree felony rape. The county then hired Special Prosecutor Greg Garrison to handle the case. Meanwhile, Tyson's promoter Don King was instrumental in retaining the famous Washington, D.C., attorney Vince Fuller to represent Tyson. Later, Harvard law professor Alan Dershowitz joined Tyson's legal team.

The defense suggested that Tyson's sexual exploits were well known and that Washington willingly consented to sex and was trying to exploit Tyson for money. Tyson testified before the jury regarding his crass nature with women. The jury's guilty verdict rested on Washington's believability as well as the significant inconsistencies in Tyson's grand jury testimony and his trial testimony. Tyson was sentenced to 10 years in prison, but served just 3 and was released in March 1995.

The Profile

High School

Mike Tyson was born in the Bedford-Stuyvesant section of Brooklyn, where he lived with his mother and two siblings until they moved to

Brownsville when he was 10 years old. Although Tyson never knew his father, he was accustomed to the sporadic presence of his mother's live-in boyfriend. Growing up in one of the most crime-infested neighborhoods in New York, Tyson also saw a significant amount of violence in his home, where his mother was physically abused by her boyfriend.

After moving to Brownsville, Mike became a street thug involved in picking pockets, stealing jewelry, mugging people, and holding up stores. Because of his abnormal size at his young age, older teenage gangsters brought Mike along on their crime sprees. "Like the check-cashing place and the supermarket," Tyson told *Sports Illustrated*. "They held the guns. I would just put everything in a bag. I was 11" (Nack, 1986, p. 27). His peer group led him down a path that increased the severity of his crimes and kept him out of school. By age 12, he was accustomed to carrying weapons and hanging around drug dealers and pimps. "[Expletive], we were wild," said Tyson. "We didn't [expletive] around, man; we were a bunch of maniacs. Sometimes we got really crazy, nuts, got guns and just started shooting in the neighborhood" (Garrison & Roberts, 1994, p. 157).

Tyson's truancy and criminal habits led the New York school system to place him in a juvenile detention center in The Bronx. After repeated failure to change his behavior, Tyson was transferred to a state facility, the Tryon School for Boys, in upstate New York, when he was 13 years old. It was here that Tyson's incredible physical stature, 5'8" and 210 lbs, was noticed by a staff member who was a former professional boxer.

Partially motivated by a visit to the school by Muhammad Ali, Tyson took an interest in boxing. Possessing only a third-grade reading level and a propensity to act violently toward other juveniles in the school, Tyson nonetheless demonstrated inconceivable physical power and determination when he was afforded an opportunity to spar with the school's boxing instructor, Jeromey Stewart. "I knew what was at the end of the rainbow—trouble and jail—but I wanted to be accepted," Tyson recalled (Nack, 1986, p. 26). For perhaps the first time in his young life, boxing offered "an alternative to crime, a socially acceptable way for Tyson to channel his rage" (Garrison & Roberts, 1994, p. 158). Thus, the former Golden Gloves champion, Jeromey Stewart, began teaching Tyson to box. Within just months, Stewart was unable to withstand Tyson's punches. "I'd have gotten killed," said Stewart. "I had to train if I was to survive" (Nack, 1986, p. 25).

Adolescent Years

Stewart was friends with one of the world's most revered boxing trainers, Cus D'Amato, who ran a boxing school just 80 miles from where Tyson was housed. Prospective boxers came from all over the country to live on D'Amato's school grounds and train to become professional fighters. Boxing students stayed in a 14-room mansion on a 10-acre piece of property overlooking the Hudson River. Stewart made special arrangements for Tyson to be driven to Catskill so that D'Amato could observe him sparring. Despite the fact that Tyson had been arrested 38 times, D'Amato offered him a home and a shot at the title (Borges, 1992). "If you want to stay here, and if you want to listen, you could be the world heavyweight champion someday" (Nack, 1986, p. 26).

A former boxing champion and friend of Tyson's, Jose Torres recalled the pleasurable shock D'Amato felt when he first witnessed Tyson display his punching ability. "When Cus first saw Mike spar with me he seemed to be in shock," said Torres. "'This boy cannot be twelve as I've been told. Not with those moves; not with that quickness'. You could see that he was doubtful but hoping to be wrong" (Garrison & Rogers, 1994, p. 159). In a 12-year-old body, D'Amato saw "raw material he could mold into another heavyweight champion of the world: an angry, distrustful, violent kid who had the reflexes and power of a great athlete" (Garrison & Rogers, 1994, p. 159).

D'Amato obtained legal custody of Tyson, and suddenly Mike went from juvenile detention to an enormous house in the country where he had his own room, spending money, home cooked meals, and nothing to do but train to become the heavyweight champion of the world. His new environment was in stark contrast to the one he grew up in at Brownsville, New York. He now enjoyed limitless freedom as opposed to the confinement he was accustomed to in the Tryon School for Boys.

In addition to his newfound liberty, for the first time Tyson began to experience excessive verbal encouragement. Unaccustomed to receiving compliments from anyone, Tyson was now adored by the adult figures whom he had previously despised. Individuals in the Catskill community were overly gracious to him because they knew he was a potential champion in the making. "He [Tyson] saw his name in the Catskill papers when he started winning, and he liked that," said Tyson's trainer Teddy Atlas. "He saw people liking him who were pillars of society.

Regular people would talk to him, and he wanted to keep that" (Borges, 1992, p. 53).

His trainer recalled Mike saying to him, prior to his first amateur fight at age 15, "I come [*sic*] a long way, remember? Everybody likes me. I'm proud of myself. I come a long way." The trainer affirmed, "He was afraid to lose because people wouldn't like him anymore. He never had any positive feedback in any other way but boxing because he was always in trouble" (Borges, 1992, p. 53).

The customized treatment Tyson received from his teacher reinforced the concept that his fighting ability gave him license to act as he pleased without consequence. "Normally Cus was very disciplined with his boys," said Torres, who also trained under D'Amato. "He allowed no [insubordination]. But he treated Mike differently because Mike was different. He knew Mike was going to be heavyweight champion of the world. And that promise carried privileges and excused behavior" (Garrison & Roberts, 1994, p. 162). For example, Torres recalled the following incident involving Tyson and his first conditioning coach, Teddy Atlas:

> Atlas was a disciplinarian who believed that all of Cus's fighters should have to follow the same set of rules. It bothered him that D'Amato used one standard for the other fighters and another—or none—for Tyson. In 1982, Atlas's twelve-year-old sister-in-law told him that Tyson had fondled her. . . . Atlas confronted Tyson in the gym. Aiming a gun at Tyson's head, Atlas told the sixteen-year-old boxer that if he ever touched his sister-in-law again, he was dead. Several weeks later, D'Amato dismissed Atlas. Again, the message to Tyson was clear: Do what you want. You're special. (Garrison & Roberts, 1994, p. 163)

Throughout his teenage years, Tyson's superiors chose to overlook his occasional violent episodes that spilled outside of the ring. The assurance that Tyson would one day sit atop the sport of boxing was far too great a likelihood to jeopardize in the interest of curtailing his aggressive tendencies. "Cus wanted to engineer a champion," Torres said (Garrison & Roberts, 1994, p. 159). Tyson's socially deplorable conduct was an essential facet of his unique nature that would make him the most destructive boxer in the world.

Professional

Before his nineteenth birthday, Mike Tyson received an $850,000 contract from ABC-TV to participate in four fights (Nack, 1986). Having never been employed in his life, Tyson obtained instant wealth. By age 19, he had completed 15 professional fights—all of them victories and 11 of them by first-round knockouts (Nack, 1986). Without question, he was the most disciplined fighter in the world. "He has no control of his emotions outside the ring," said Torres. "The irony is he has so much control inside the ring" (Borges, 1992, p. 53). Largely due to an absence of self-responsibility, Tyson employed a full-time companion whose primary function was menial tasks such as carrying his driver's license and keys, reminding him of his schedule, and monitoring the women who surrounded him.

After becoming the youngest heavyweight champion in the world, Tyson's insulation from social responsibility was fortified. Within 5 years of turning pro, he earned over $50 million, purchased a 27,000 square foot mansion and acquired a Lamborghini, two Mercedes, a Rolls-Royce, two Porsches, two Ferraris, and a Range Rover (Borges, 1992).

His championship status made him the most celebrated athlete in the world, and Tyson admitted, "I could pee on the street and someone would pat me on the back" (Borges, 1992, p. 53). His repeated escapes from the consequences of unlawful acts made him fully aware of his exemption from the law. In 1988, he exited an 8-month marriage to actress Robin Givens, who had accused him of physical abuse. "She really pissed me off, so I hit her with a kind of backhand punch," Tyson admitted to Torres. "Jose, she hit every [expletive] wall in the room. It was a great punch. And then she wanted to call the cops from my own [expletive] telephone. My own telephone" (Garrison & Roberts, 1994, p. 164).

Later that same year, Tyson was involved in a well-publicized street fight in Harlem, as well as several car accidents. None of this infringed on his fighting and promotion schedule. Perhaps the closest form of discipline he received followed an incident at a nightclub where he accosted a woman. After she resisted his advances, Tyson said to her, "You bitch. You don't know who I am? I'm Mike Tyson, the heavyweight champion of the world. Who the hell do you think you are? Celebrities slobber all over me. You're not even that pretty. You're nobody" (Borges, 1992, p. 53). He was convicted of battery, but served no jail time. The victim received $100 (Borges, 1992).

The Access

Despite Tyson's storied history of deviant behavior, some women made themselves available to him nonetheless. "All these women, they don't want me," Tyson admitted. "They want my cash or to be seen with me" (Borges, 1992, p. 53). Tyson's fancy for women, and more specifically sex, was no secret. His sparring partner Torres insisted that Tyson was unable to control his lust for sex, which was a dangerous condition considering the unlimited availability of women at his disposal.

Torres recalled one occasion where Tyson had sexual intercourse with 24 women in a single night (Borges, 1992). It was this kind of hyperfascination with sex that led to countless charges by women that Tyson had fondled them. Further, there were women who allegedly gave birth to illegitimate children fathered by Tyson, and a history of civil suits against him ranged from rape to sexual harassment.

The degree to which women had been reduced to disposable vessels in the eyes of Mike Tyson is best summed up by the following account from an NFL player who attended a party at which Tyson was present:

> He walks in there and go [sic], "I've got to get some pussy, got to get some pussy." Now, I've been around a lot of people, but nobody comes in there with the proudness that they feel that they're that macho that they can just, you know, it's like a drink, an item. There's no feeling behind it. It's just something, you know, that I've got to physically conquer. (personal interview, 1994)

The Incident

In July 1991, the city of Indianapolis was hosting an annual festival celebrating black culture. Some of the promoters of Black Expo had arranged for Mike Tyson to make an appearance at the beauty pageant. Getting the heavyweight champion of the world to show up at the event was a coup because of the massive publicity he generated for the entire affair.

After arriving in town on the evening prior to his scheduled appearance at the Expo, Tyson visited two Indianapolis nightclubs in the company of rap singer B Angie B. After spending the evening together in his suite, they awoke midway through the morning, had sex, and went back to sleep. A short time later, they awoke and again engaged in intercourse before getting out of bed around noon. She had a concert performance to prepare for at the Hoosier Dome that evening, whereas Tyson was scheduled to pose with beauty contestants. In addition to the sexual foray with B. Angie B., Tyson's limousine driver later testified of far greater numbers of women going up to his hotel during his short stay in Indianapolis. "Oh my goodness," she recalled, "he's had so many girls up there." The female driver said that Tyson even "tried to do something to me. He tried to rip my clothes off" (Garrison & Roberts, 1994, p. 28).

According to Tyson, when he arrived at the Miss Black America rehearsal, the contestants "went crazy. They started getting excited, screaming. I started walking. I walked toward them. They surrounded me, jumped on me, touched me, saying hi, kissed me, hugged me, jumped; you know, they got excited" (Garrison & Roberts, 1994, p. 13).

Washington, an 18-year-old contestant who had just graduated from high school a month earlier, was as excited as everyone else. As did most other pageant contestants, Washington had the opportunity to pose with Tyson during a filmed promotion. Her father was a big Mike Tyson fan, therefore she hoped to get an autograph or picture with him. To her amazement, when Tyson stopped near her while making his way down the contestant line, he asked, "Would you like to go out on a date later on?" (Garrison & Roberts, 1994, p. 14). Later in the promotion, Tyson saw Washington again and asked, "The date's still on, isn't it?" (Garrison & Roberts, 1994, p. 15). This time he wrote down Desiree's room number.

That evening many of the beauty contestants attended B Angie B's concert. Tyson was also in attendance, but he and Washington did not come in contact at any time during the show. Washington returned to her hotel after the concert and was asleep when she and one of her roommates were awakened by a phone call at 1:30 a.m. Tyson's bodyguard, Dale Edwards, was calling from a limousine that was parked in front of the hotel where the contestants where staying. Because Washington had already removed her makeup and was in her pajamas, she resisted the idea of going out so late. After a second call, this time from Tyson himself,

Desiree's roommate suggested that this was a once-in-a-lifetime opportunity. Meanwhile, Tyson persisted, "Can you come out? We'll just go around. I just want to talk to you. Can you come out?" (Garrison & Roberts, 1994, p. 222).

Taking 10 minutes to dress, Washington rushed down to the hotel parking lot with her camera and climbed into Tyson's limousine. Washington's hotel was right around the corner from where Tyson was staying and he indicated that he wanted to stop by his suite to pick up some things and an additional bodyguard. With little thought, she agreed. She later testified that the entrance into the hotel lobby with Tyson was a glamorous moment. She recalled well-wishers reaching out to touch Tyson and concluded, "That was great" (Garrison & Roberts, 1994, p. 25).

Once inside his room, they engaged in friendly conversation and Tyson showed her around his luxurious suite. The discussion abruptly changed from Rhode Island and pigeons to sexual inferences when Tyson said, "You're turning me on" (Garrison & Roberts, 1994, p. 223). Washington testified to the following events at trial: "I just got really nervous and started babbling. And I said, 'I need to use your bathroom. When I come out, I want to see Indianapolis like you said'" (Garrison & Roberts, 1994, p. 223). Further, she testified that when she exited the bathroom, Tyson was sitting on the edge of his bed with nothing on except his underpants. "I was terrified," she testified. "I said, 'It's time for me to leave.' [He said] 'Come here.' And he grabbed my arm; and he was like, 'Don't fight me. Come here.' And then he stuck his tongue in my mouth. He was disgusting" (Garrison & Roberts, 1994, p. 223).

Although Washington pleaded, "I don't do one night stands and you don't have a condom on and leave me alone, I have a future ahead of me. I, you know, you're going to get me pregnant if you don't get away from me." He proceeded to force himself on her and countered with, "Don't fight me. Don't fight me. Just relax. Don't fight me. You can't win. Don't fight me. Just relax" (Garrison & Roberts, 1994, p. 27).

After forcibly committing an act of oral sex on her, he forced his penis inside her while saying, "Oh, Mommy, Mommy, come on, Mommy, come on. Don't fight me Mommy, come on, Mommy, Mommy, Mommy" (Garrison & Roberts, 1994, p. 28).

Trying in vain to stop his advances, Desiree cried and at the last instant, Tyson withdrew from Washington and ejaculated on the bed. "You're welcome to stay the night if you want," said Tyson, seemingly oblivious to the trauma that he had just inflicted (Garrison & Roberts, 1994, p. 28). Washington hastily gathered up her clothes and scampered out of the room. The following day she checked into Methodist Hospital in Indianapolis where she underwent a rape-kit examination. The attending physician detected two abrasions on the opening to Washington's vagina but was unable to complete the exam because when he attempted to probe further, "Desiree cried out in pain and almost backed off the table" (Garrison & Roberts, 1994, p. 179). After discussing it with her parents, Washington went to the Indianapolis police and pressed charges against Mike Tyson for rape.

The Court's Response

Jurisdiction

After listening to Washington's statement regarding her alleged assault at the hands of Tyson, sex-crimes investigator Tommy Kuzmik concluded that she was an excellent witness. When he first reported to Marion County district attorney Jeff Modisett, Kuzmik flatly indicated that Tyson had raped Washington. Typical of any acquaintance rape case, Modisett's concern was whether there was sufficient evidence to gain a conviction. Moreover, Tyson's status presented a host of problems not found in run-of-the-mill rape complaints. The task of carrying out an investigation with the crush of reporters converging on Indianapolis would be a detriment to gathering crucial evidence in the case. Because they considered the case to be as strong as any the office had ever prosecuted, the county went ahead with a full investigation.

The investigation was impossible to hide from the press, and the district attorney was quickly faced with a decision to either charge Tyson and issue a warrant for his arrest or convene a special grand jury to determine if there was probable cause to indict. A special grand jury was impaneled, and after hearing Washington, Tyson, and other witnesses testify, they voted to indict Tyson for felony rape.

Assembly of Lawyers

Tyson's promoter, Don King, was wealthier than the champ and had had his share of personal experience in criminal court. He quickly secured a national defense team of lawyers led by Washington, D.C., attorney Vince Fuller. Fuller had successfully defended John Hinckley, Jr., on the charge of attempted murder on President Reagan. He was retained for $500 per hour. Tyson had no role in the selection of his legal representation. "Don said these were good guys," said Tyson. "I didn't know anything" ("Mike Tyson Speaks," 1994, p. 39). In addition, Harvard law professor Alan Dershowitz was hired to prepare the appeal in the event that Tyson was convicted.

The Athlete's Perception of the Incident

The initial news of the investigation into rape charges against Tyson invoked an attitude of little concern from Don King's lawyer, who said, "We hear the same kind of thing about once a month. Mike is a target for just about anyone who wants to take a shot at him" (personal interview, 1994). Because King has the reputation to attract instant national media attention, Tyson was defended and Washington was smeared in the theater of public opinion even before grand jury testimony began. Once in Indianapolis, Tyson's account came forward.

Tyson testified before the grand jury that he had engaged in sexual intercourse with Washington and that the affair was entirely consensual. After all, the accuser had given her hotel room phone number to Tyson, received his 1:30 a.m. phone call, voluntarily gotten into his limousine at two o'clock in the morning and received a kiss on the cheek from him, accompanied him to his hotel, and willfully went to his bedroom. All of these actions were terribly consistent with the legions of other women who had gone to bed with Tyson for the sole purpose of having sex with one of the most famous athletes in the world.

In terms of all these factors contributing to Tyson's perception that Washington was consenting to sex, Dershowitz stated, "It probably was a factor in his mind. She appeared to be consenting. It sounds to me like he thought she was going to consent, not that she had consented but that she was going to consent." Tyson testified to his belief that she went with him specifically for sex. "I believe that we had both made it clear earlier that day what was going to happen, and that she came to my room at 2 o'clock in the morning. I'm sure we made it clear" said Tyson (*Michael G. Tyson v. State of Indiana*, 1992, p. 43).

Lawyers' Strategy

The Obstacles

Although virtually all acquaintance rape cases are reduced to a he-said-she said test of believability, the state's evidence against Tyson was unusually weighted in the prosecution's favor. Forensic evidence included injuries that supported Washington's claim that she had been forcibly penetrated. Expert opinion suggested that the abrasions to Washington's vaginal area were inconsistent with consensual sex, thus refuting Tyson's insistence that Washington welcomed his sexual advances. Finally, Tyson's alibi conflicted sharply with the host of witnesses whose testimony endorsed the credibility of Washington's rendition of events that evening. Further, grand jury testimony revealed that Tyson's chief witness, his personal bodyguard, lied about being in the suite during the alleged rape. It was also discovered that Tyson's bodyguard had a prior perjury conviction, thus casting further doubt on the reliability of his initial account, which coincided with Tyson's explanation of the events that evening.

With all the various forms of evidence strongly pointing toward Tyson's guilt, only one viable defense tactic remained—character and witness credibility. Whereas character evidence presented in rape cases against athletes usually involves an aggressive discrediting of the accuser by portraying her as a disreputable sex-seeking groupie, the defense opted to veer from this strategy. Unlike numerous women who had accused Tyson of aggressive sexual behavior in the past, Washington had a reputation that lent believability to her account. She was an unknown high school graduate who was the recipient of the Martin Luther King scholarship. She was also,

> Freshman class president, National Honors Society member, varsity cheerleader, member of the high school softball team, recipient of the Outstanding High School Student Award from her school, . . . one of thirty-four high school students chosen to represent the United States on a summer tour of the USSR in 1990, she had met with Soviet diplomats and officials, Vice President Dan Quayle, and American business and church leaders. She was active in church and charity affairs: Big Sisters to three-year-old foster child, member of the

Senior Teens Aid for the Retarded program." (Garrison & Roberts, 1994, pp. 13-14)

Her background was wholly inconsistent with that of a sports groupie who typically pursues athletes and engages in promiscuous sex. Washington had never been with a professional athlete. Her pristine background clashed sharply with that of a groupie.

On the other hand, Tyson approached the courtroom with a storied history that included domestic abuse, alleged sexual assault, and sexual harassment. He had been through a sensational divorce with Robin Givens after she disclosed on national television that he had beaten her. With Givens by his side, Tyson did not deny her vivid account of his violent outbursts. Tyson had also been convicted for battery against a woman in Manhattan, and settled out of court with another woman for fondling her. Further, he had been the subject of numerous other civil suits of a sexual nature.

With a reputable accuser alleging that she had been raped by a famous athlete, Tyson's lawyers deviated from the typical practice of honing in on the sports-groupie image and instead opted to highlight the sexually obsessive athlete. By exposing the jury to the sexual indulgences of Tyson with a backdrop of Washington's well-educated background, the defense suggested that it was unreasonable to suppose that a woman of Washington's intelligence was unaware that Tyson intended to have sex with her when she agreed to enter his hotel room at two o'clock in the morning. The implication was that Washington was a coy, savvy woman who slept with Tyson for personal gain.

Although this strategy would still subject her to some of the character attack that rape complainants typically undergo, Washington's character came under far greater scrutiny. "Mike Tyson was a touching, grabbing, heat-seeking sex machine; all women knew this and avoided him if they didn't want to become part of his collection of sex toys," said Special Prosecutor, Greg Garrison. "Ergo, since Desiree Washington was a woman and didn't avoid him, she must have known what a 'date' with Tyson entailed" (personal interview, 1994).

Witness after witness took the stand for the defense and revealed Tyson's crass sexual mannerisms that qualified as an obsession. The following is a sample of some of the testimony from various women who were called by the defense to describe Tyson's sexual forwardness at the Expo:

You want to come to my room? You want to party? I know
I'm not going to get none from you, but I'm going to ask
anyway.

[Referring to a "southern girl" who likes to cook] That's
good, because I like to eat; and I'm not talking about food.

If you don't want to go out with me, I could move on,
because I could have any one of those bitches out there.

I know you want me. I want to [expletive] you, and bring
your roommate too, because I'm a celebrity, and, you know,
we do that kind of thing.

Everything he said had a sexual overtone to it. And most
of the times he was just totally blunt. . . . He said . . . "Do you
want to go out?" . . . "We can do it here and then back to my
room for sex or a kiss. A kiss will do. Sex would be better."
(Garrison & Roberts, 1994, p. 246)

After having numerous women verify the boxer's obviously distorted
perception of women, Tyson took the stand in his own defense and
fortified the women's portrait of himself. He admitted on the stand,
"That's kind of bold. That's the way I am, I just want to know what I'm
getting before I get into it" (Garrison & Roberts, 1994, p. 250). Having
enlightened a jury of common citizens to the sexual indulgences available
within the confines of celebrity athletics, Fuller argued, "I submit to you,
it insults your intelligence to be led to believe that a young woman of
this woman's background, her sophistication, would get into the back of
a limousine, be hugged and be kissed on the mouth and not leave that
car forthwith unless she knew what was coming" (Garrison & Roberts,
1994, p. 265).

The failure to attempt to link the accuser's conduct with the actions
of sports groupies played a critical role in the jury's eventual finding of
guilt. Dershowitz, after taking up Tyson's appeal, reflected, "Had I been
the defense lawyer in this case, I would have focused on the groupie
phenomenon and would have concluded that Desiree Washington was a
groupie. And certainly she acted like a groupie. She behaved like a
groupie" (personal interview, 1995). During the appeal process, he
successfully employed this approach and elicited doubt in the general
public over the verdict. More importantly, his style even contributed to
six members of the jury publicly reversing their original guilty vote [see
Appeal section following].

Victim's Motive

Without the asset of having an accuser profiled as a less than respectable woman who had previously engaged in promiscuous behavior, the defense was left to imply that Washington's accusation against Tyson was financially motivated and rooted in her bitterness over being cavalierly discarded after a one-night stand. Fuller argued before the jury:

> I submit Miss Washington suddenly realized that she's been treated like a one-night stand or worse, and her dignity is offended. . . . Mr. Tyson's behavior, no doubt, was rude in his treatment of Miss Washington after their sexual encounter. She is a woman of great pride, of great achievement. And now she feels she's been treated like a one-night stand. (Garrison & Roberts, 1994, p. 266)

The suggestion that Washington was "embarrassed and humiliated" and driven by revenge was combined with the accusation that Tyson's wealth was the substance behind the rape claim. Under cross-examination, Washington was asked numerous questions relating to money, such as whether or not she sang the song "For the Love of Money" after meeting Tyson the first time. Furthermore, she was questioned about an alleged retainer between her lawyer and her parents, the implication being that there was an orchestrated plan to bilk the publicity surrounding the case for financial gain.

These insinuations had little impact on the jury and were later disproved entirely after the conclusion of the trial when Washington agreed to appear on ABC's "20/20" as well as on the cover of *People* magazine, both without receiving any money. Perhaps the piece of evidence that most strongly refuted the suggestion that Washington was a gold digger came from the revelation that she had been offered $1 million to drop the charges against Tyson just prior to trial (Berkow, 1992). She declined the offer.

Disposition

The immediate challenge faced by the prosecution in this case was overcoming the jury's inclination to question the behavior of a woman who willfully went to the room of an established sex fiend at two o'clock in the morning. The prosecutor knew that even before Washington had a chance to testify, jurors—particularly the female jurors—would likely be skeptical of her actions. "The first thing out of their mouths was 'I wouldn't put myself in that position,' " said one male juror, referring to the female jurors (personal interview, 1994). Although the female jurors were convinced that it had been a bad decision to go to Mike Tyson's room at two o'clock in the morning, Washington herself did not recognize her folly until after the fact. Garrison described how Tyson's celebrity-athlete status magnified the victim's guilt in this case, thus contributing to the difficulty in trying this case before a jury:

> Self-blame is pretty consistent in every case. I think it is worse when it involves an athlete because not only are you a dumb ass for going out with the wrong guy, but you're really a dumb ass for not knowing a jock was going to try to get you.
>
> I know that Desiree struggled awful hard with "Well, how could he be like that because he's Mike Tyson? And my dad idolizes him." So it's not just Joe-the-Ragman that she had a date with. Well everybody knows that jocks have got one idea on their mind all the time. Except then you see him and "There he is. Gosh, he's famous. Oh wow. He's a hero." Boom! (personal interview, 1994)

The prosecution demonstrated that 18-year-old Washington was star struck by the thought of having a date with her father's sports idol. Although she welcomed the opportunity to orbit a famous celebrity, she was clearly distinguishable from a sports groupie who positioned herself around an athlete in hopes of having sex with him.

The jury was able to separate her behavior from the countless women who had pursued Tyson in the past. "I think she was star struck," said one juror. "If Tyson was a household name due to her father, she could go home afterward and say, 'Hey, Tyson kissed me.' Her father would say, 'Yea? Hey terrific. I'm glad it happened.' With Tyson being a celebrity, it's no big deal" (personal interview, 1994).

As the trial progressed, jurors accepted her behavior primarily because they believed Washington was sincere. She did not project as a sports groupie. "All of us thought she was credible," said one juror, despite the fact that she voluntarily went to Tyson's room (personal interview, 1994). Jurors viewed Washington's attitude toward Tyson as inconsistent with that of a groupie. "Some of the contestants that testified said that she was friendly, but she wasn't the groupie type," insisted one juror. "When Tyson came around, you know, when he got close to her, she didn't fall all over him. That type of stuff" (personal interview, 1994).

Even though the defense exerted great effort to portray Tyson as a rude, crass, sexual athlete, the jury did not convict him for his base manner. One juror confirmed that even the female jurors were not offended by Tyson's admission of sexual forwardness. Their collective attitude was that his sex life was his own business. Thus, the defense's decision to focus on Tyson while remaining reluctant to scrutinize the victim left the jury with an untainted portrait of a likable, believable teenager who was abused by a predator.

"I thought she was very intelligent," said one juror. "She didn't seem like the type of person who went to parties straight just for sex. She was like me. If there was a celebrity around who I liked, I'd go" (personal interview, 1994).

Jurors formed their opinions of Washington on the basis of what was revealed in court. "The questions she was asked about her background," said one juror, referring to the how she came to find her believable. "What she was doing then. The things that she had did [*sic*] for the government. I guess she had been in Washington and some of the pageants she had been in. It wasn't like she was doing it because she was sexy" (personal interview, 1994).

The juror further explained that Washington was not sexually moti-vated. "I just didn't think that that was a type of person who just ran around with everybody she met," he said (personal interview, 1994).

Moreover, Tyson's excessive indulgence in illicit behavior persuaded the jurors that he was capable of raping someone. His insistence that he did not need to resort to rape due to an abundance of women at his disposal did not convince them. The juror explained,

> He was used to going to bed with somebody different every night. After a while, you get used to it. And he'd been with Ms. B Angie B about three hours before this. All of these women are willing. So when a woman says "no," his attitude is "To hell with what this bitch says. You know, I'm famous. I'm Mike Tyson. Who's going to tell anybody what hap-pened?" (personal interview, 1994)

Although Tyson's world permitted him to indulge in inconceivable amounts of consensual sexual encounters without any repercussions, the law does not consider his sexual conditioning as an excuse to force himself on a woman or mistakenly assume that any woman who goes with him is consenting to sex. As one juror said,

> He's been with all these other women and they've wanted it. Why should [Washington] be any different? And maybe in his mind he didn't think he was doing it, but I mean the law says, "If this lady says 'no' and tries to fight you, you're guilty of rape whether you think you are or not." (personal interview, 1994)

Convicted on one count of rape and two counts of criminal deviant conduct, Tyson was sentenced to concurrent terms of 10 years on each count. Four years were suspended.

The Appeal

The appeal process provided an opportunity for Dershowitz to amend the trial lawyers' failure to exploit the groupie factor during the trial. Had this case been approached from the outset as another consenting groupie trying to exploit a rich, famous athlete, there would have been far greater doubt to be cast on jurors' minds regarding Washington's credibility. As soon as Dershowitz assumed control of the appeal, a reconstructed theory of the case emerged that suggested Tyson had been victimized by a gold-digging groupie who sexually exploited a celebrity. As Dershowitz said later,

> My own sense is that she was prepared to use sex as a way of getting more than just a one-night stand with Mike Tyson. And she wanted his money. That was her goal from the beginning. She said to her friend that she wanted his money. And she couldn't get it by the first route so she decided to go the second route. The second route was crying rape. (personal interview, 1995)

Attempting to transform Washington into a promiscuous liar who had hoodwinked the jury, Dershowitz laced his appeals brief with unsupported sexual innuendo about her. The brief to the Indiana Court of Appeals referred to Washington giving Tyson a picture of herself in a bathing suit, "posed with her hand on her hip and her chest thrust forward" (*Michael G. Tyson v. State of Indiana*, 1992, p. 3). It went on to describe her as a woman with an appetite for sex. Recounting her meeting with Tyson at the rehearsal, Tyson's lawyers wrote,

> When she had her picture taken, posed in Tyson's lap, she stared at him, sat there longer than the other girls, and seemed more engrossed in him. She had to be pried off of him. She was very "deliberate" in her interaction with Tyson . . . with her eyes wide, and her mouth open.

The brief went as far as to allege that "Washington speculated about the size of his penis" (*Michael G. Tyson v. State of Indiana*, 1992, p. 7).

The brief further alleged,

> When Washington first met Tyson, she behaved like a typical groupie. She met Tyson later, under circumstances which suggested an interest in sex—she accepted an invitation at 1:40 a.m., voluntarily accompanied Tyson to his hotel room, and willingly sat on his bed with him. (*Michael G. Tyson v. State of Indiana*, 1992, p. 44)

In the brief, Dershowitz and his colleagues alleged that during her attendance at the B. Angie B. concert, Desiree "had gone backstage, looking for celebrities . . . acting like 'groupies'" (*Michael G. Tyson v. State of Indiana*, 1992, p. 5).

In addition to the petitions filed with the various appeals courts, Washington became the focus of a cover story in *Penthouse Magazine*, one of the world's leading pornographic magazines for men (Dershowitz, 1993). Dershowitz, a regular contributor to *Penthouse*, authored the article entitled "The Rape of Mike Tyson." In the scurrilous article, Dershowitz further sexualized Washington by suggesting that she had previously engaged in sexual intercourse with another athlete—a high school football player. "She falsely accused somebody of rape once before and used a false accusation to try to get herself out of a problem with her father which we submit is what happened here," he said (personal interview, 1995). But this sensational claim was never proven. Nonetheless, Dershowitz insisted on discussing it. He said,

Desiree Washington's prior sexual experience, it seems to me, is much more relevant on this issue. . . . [G]iven a choice between having his whole sex life and her whole sex life in front of the jury, or none, I prefer to have it all from Tyson's point of view. Because I think we can explain his sex life. He's not on trial for his sex life. He's on trial for rape. Whereas she falsely accused somebody of rape. That's very relevant. (personal interview, 1995)

While portraying Washington as a sexual groupie, Dershowitz insisted her false rape claim was financially motivated. He maintained that the trial verdict would have been different had they heard all the evidence with respect to her character:

They might have come to a conclusion . . . that she wasn't anxious to have sex with him but was willing to have sex with him if she thought that was necessary to become his friend and his lover and perhaps his wife. That she never said "no," but was coy—but went along with it. (personal interview, 1995)

Dershowitz's aggressive tact successfully sowed seeds of doubt in the former jurors' minds. After being exposed to Dershowitz's claims, six jurors publicly recanted their verdict. He had skillfully deflected attention away from the evidence, thereby shifting public opinion about the accuracy of the trial outcome.

Nonetheless, his publicity stunts failed in court. He was unsuccessful in convincing the appeals court to order a new trial. Although the jurors' change of heart after the fact is not recognized by the appeals court as ample grounds to retry the case, the easy turn of opinion demonstrates the powerful persuasion of the groupie defense.

5

Final Thoughts

In light of existing research regarding predictive behavior for perpetrators of sexual assault, the link between star athletes and incidents of sexual assault is significant. Alan Berkowitz (1992) has succinctly summarized perpetrator characteristics that increase the potential for males to perpetrate acquaintance rape and other forms of sexual assault (I will be referring to his summary throughout this chapter). Berkowitz's three key predictors—male socialization, attitudes and personality characteristics, and early sexual experiences—to professional athletes' peculiar social experience suggests an exaggerated likelihood for "rape-supportive attitudes and beliefs" to be held and reinforced.

Berkowitz cited Brannon and David's research to identify specific components of male socialization that "predispose [men] to dominate and abuse women" (Berkowitz, 1992). It is generally accepted by scholars that American culture supports male behavior that encourages men to distance themselves from feminine perceptions; encourages quests for power, status, and control; refuses to show emotion (e.g., acting tough) and approves of aggression. Whereas these credos may be advertised and promoted to the society at large, they are intricately woven into the prerequisites of successful participation in aggressive sports. The following statements from one of the professional athletes whom I interviewed suggests a relation between the above characteristics and employment in a revenue-generating sport:

Professional athletes are people who have done a lot to deny
a lot of feelings because to be a professional athlete you have
to deny a lot of feeling. You have to deny a lot of physical
pain. You have to deny a lot of emotional pain. You have to
overcome a great deal of adversity—physically and emotion-
ally. You have to deal with moving to places you may not be
familiar with and being around people you may not be
familiar with. Separation from your family constantly. So
there's a lot of things that you do deny yourself. A lot
of athletes deny themselves the pain of making the right
decision—of the discomfort, I should say, of making the right
decision.

You lie to yourself about how good you are in what you
do. If you have to go up against Michael Jordan, you gonna
[*sic*] tell yourself, "I can play Michael Jordan." You have to
because the minute you doubt yourself you're done. He's by
you.

So players may be at a point where they say, "Well, she
probably doesn't want to have sex, but I'm so good she's
gonna [*sic*] love this." Because that's what you tell yourself.
(personal interview, 1995)

Berkowitz (1992) added that "sex role socialization provides men
with permission to commit sexual abuse and creates a cognitive framework that allows them to justify similar behavior among male peers."
The athlete-groupie relationship epitomizes a situation where males feel
justified in sexually exploiting women. The ability to indulge in the
constant presence of women who surrender their bodies for sex, all the
while being held in such high esteem by society, grants athletes the
opportunity and the permission to act sexually without restraint. The
athlete-groupie relationship guarantees a purely sexual encounter free of
consequence, commitment, or responsibility.

Existing in an atmosphere where demonstrated masculinity is an
occupational necessity, players who dabble in the groupie scene are
provided with exceptional opportunities to relate their sexual conquests
as evidence of manliness. Berkowitz pointed out that a constant affirm-
ation of one's masculinity is expressed "in conversations with other men
[who] frequently emphasize their sexual experience" One NFL player
insisted that the need to publicly reaffirm one's manhood is paramount
in NFL locker rooms:

> Players share information. You talk about conquest, conquest
> of women. The sports environment has excluded women. It
> is male dominated and it's about winning. So what do you
> do? You see guys talking trash, "I'm going to take you deep,"
> meaning in football "I'm going to catch the long pass on you."
> They talk trash all the time. They have to talk trash about
> their game on the field. You know they have to talk trash about
> their game in the bedroom. (personal interview, 1994)

Despite denials by Cincinnati Bengals players that any discussion
took place among them following their encounter with Victoria C., one
defendant conceded that significant bragging took place in the locker
room for days afterward. Moreover, the tales grew more colorful as they
were retold.

The safety zone afforded players, in which they are free to act out
sexually without recourse, fortifies beliefs that decriminalize rape in the
perpetrators' minds. Berkowitz (1992) suggested that "as a result of their
socialization experiences, men may develop attitudes and belief systems
that allow them to justify sexual assault or not to define it as such." The
framework within which athletes and some women engage in multiple,
serial sexual encounters accelerates the formation of beliefs among some
athletes that sexual assault is mere recreation. One defendant in the
Bengals case referred to the alleged rape as "a human act." He insisted,
"It wasn't brutality. It was in fun, enjoyment, not as in brutality or
something that could be classified as even criminal" (personal interview,
1994).

For athletes so inclined, the sheer number of sexual encounters with
different partners validates a purely sexual function for women. Conse-
quently, some athletes lose sight of any line between consent and force.

With respect to the third perpetrator characteristic—personality
characteristics and early sexual experience—Berkowitz (1992) stated,
"Other researchers have found sexually coercive behavior to be associated with characteristics of irresponsibility, lack of social conscience
and values legitimizing aggression against women," among other things.
These findings assume added significance in light of the excessive levels
of social irresponsibility and inconsequential behavior that are often
found among high-profile athletes. For celebrated athletes, there is a
steady stripping away of accountability that corresponds with increased
popularity. This widens the latitude athletes have to act without conse-

quence. Their excessive wealth and public admiration insulates them from the social accountability required of most citizens.

Beginning in high school, the path to athletic stardom is furnished with what Berkowitz described as a "support for a developmental sequence of sexual aggression . . . serving as preconditions of sexual violence in the presence of facilitating environmental conditions."

Whereas the athlete-groupie behavior framework involves women who willfully enter relationships that will require them to submit to potentially degrading circumstances, the practice also substantially increases the risk for potential sexual assaults against women who are not groupies. One result is the occurrence of women naively traversing the boundaries of the athletes' culture. The mere presence of a woman at a popular social hangout where athletes and groupies congregate can be enough to activate an athlete's conditioning toward sex. Discussing "situational risk factors," Berkowitz said that "attitudes and belief systems about sexuality . . . may be triggered by actual situations that are interpreted as justifying sexual intimacy." The more extensive an athlete's involvement with groupies, the more narrow his view of women in general. The constant confirmation of women as disposable sex objects establishes a belief system that identifies all female social contacts as fair sexual game.

Referring to "another set of risk factors for sexual assault," Berkowitz summarized that, "situations or characteristics of dates that have been empirically correlated with sexual assault include those associated with men's increased control or dominance (such as date location and activity, who initiates and who pays, and . . . the nature of the victim-perpetrator relationship)." The circumstances that precede sexual encounters for some athletes entail a woman seeking out the athlete, tacitly or overtly yielding her body to his desires as a prerequisite to gaining his company, accompanying him to his hotel room, and being dismissed soon after completing intercourse.

One member of the Bengals said the following about one of his teammates who was a defendant in the rape case:

> He had a certain dominance. He felt a certain dominance over women. He felt he had power over them. He had them in control. They are easy to pick up. They are easy to manipulate. They are just easy to get the things you want out of them.

> Being an athlete you get notoriety, wealth and power. He was a person who used his. He used it to the fullest. I mean, he had the wealth. He had this very plush, gorgeous home. He had to use that power to get somebody. "Hey, I'm [name deleted] and you know I have all this stuff." And then once he got em' [*sic*] over to his house he wanted to control them. He wanted to just control her mind, her body, everything. (personal interview, 1994)

In short, the conditions under which athletes meet and engage groupies shortens the distance between socially irresponsible behavior and criminal sexual assault. Berkowitz confirmed that "an environment that promotes narrow, stereotypical conceptions of masculinity" advances the likelihood for rape (personal interview, 1994). This probability is compounded with athletes who engage groupies because their conception of women is extremely narrow and distorted as well—with women occupying an exclusively sexual role.

Solutions

The roots to sexual violence run deep and are not found in the mere participation in organized athletics. Violence against women is pervasive throughout society and is far too complex a problem for the entertainment industry to solve. But the deviant social lifestyles embraced by so many of today's high-profile athletes increases the frequency of reported incidents of sexual assault in the ranks of ballplayers. Although the sports industry cannot be expected to shoulder the task of completely eradicating the problem of athletes' violence against women, there are measures that can be taken to stem the increasing number of assaults.

Nonetheless, the sports industry has demonstrated a clear callousness toward the abuse of women by players. Repeatedly denying the presence of any particular problem among athletes, league representatives and coaches have proved to be altogether unwilling and incapable of taking any initiative to curb the problem. Moreover, the plentiful resources of teams, league front offices, and players unions are more often used to support abusive players. Thus, it is incumbent on others—colleges who recruit athletes, law enforcement, and the public—to act affirmatively to combat the frequent abuse of women by high-profile athletes.

Colleges

There needs to be a much stronger message of intolerance sent when male athletes first abuse women—long before they arrive in the professional ranks and earn millions of dollars. Many of the professional athletes who are arrested for violating women have a history of prior mistreatment of women, often reaching all the way back to high school.

Due to the unique relationship between scholarship athletes and institutions of higher learning, universities and colleges are in a position to take steps to prevent recurring abuse of women by athletes. When a college athlete is arrested or otherwise formally charged with sexually assaulting a woman, schools should immediately suspend the accused player's scholarship. This should be done prior to the school independently determining the merits of the complaint. Following the scholarship suspension, school officials can assess whether the facts warrant revoking the scholarship altogether pending the outcome of criminal proceedings.

Short of concluding—prior to the disposition of the criminal case—that the alleged sexual assault indeed occurred, school officials have sufficient grounds to revoke a scholarship if either of the following circumstances exist: (a) additional student code-of-conduct violations that do not constitute criminal conduct, but are nonetheless associated with the more serious pending sexual assault allegations; or (b) a previous record, albeit unrelated to the case at hand, of criminal misbehavior by the athlete that has led to arrest, indictment, or conviction.

An illustration is provided in a sexual assault complaint filed against five Brigham Young University (BYU) football players in 1995. After the five players were reported to the Provo, Utah, police, both civil and university officials conducted investigations. The incident involved, among other things, alcohol consumption—a violation of the school's code of conduct. With the players admitting to participating in consensual sex with the complainant, but denying the use of force, law-enforcement authorities declined to file formal charges on the basis of insufficient evidence. Nonetheless, BYU officials expelled all five athletes, despite never determining the validity of the rape allegation. Once the school's internal investigation found that the incident entailed violations of other aspects of the school's policies, the athletic department was notified that the players were no longer eligible to be on scholarship (Benedict, 1997).

Law Enforcement

Although criminal complaints against recognizable athletes represent a statistically insignificant number of the overall sexual assault complaints filed with police and prosecutors, these few cases draw the most public attention. Violence against women perpetrated by athletes tends to be a touchstone of society's larger problem with the mistreatment of women. For example, there was little public discourse about domestic violence prior to the O. J. Simpson case. This is not to say that cases against athletes deserve more attention from law enforcement. But those in position to make determinations on whether to charge an accused player should be less skeptical of complainants' accounts and more willing to subject accused athletes to vigorous investigation.

Although the law enforcement community is becoming increasingly aware of the less than exemplary attitudes and actions of star athletes, there remains a reluctance on the part of investigators to arrest players accused of sexual assault by women who appear to have initiated the relationship. Moreover, prosecutors are even more hesitant to indict on the basis of a complaint brought by an accuser who may appear to have sought out her perpetrator. Although the public's impatience with less than pure victims in acquaintance rape cases makes law enforcement's trepidation understandable on the one hand, investigators and prosecutors must nonetheless hold these male role models to the social standards contained in the law.

By failing to indict athletes accused of sexual assault, law enforcement is essentially throwing in the towel and adding to the perception of license held by many of these perpetrators. Perhaps even more damaging, the public—particularly the younger generation of sports fans—sees athletic ability being treated as an exemption pass from the demands of justice.

The Public

Ultimately, it is the public—the consumers who finance the salaries of high-priced athletes—who have the most influential power to curb

athletes' violence against women. Money is the engine driving professional sports. In order to change behavior and attitudes, the millions of
American spectators must give sports leagues an incentive to take action
against abusive players. But Americans are complacent when it comes to
watching criminal athletes as long as they perform adequately on the
field. There is little moral resolve to resist paying to see and cheering
for athletes who are abusive to women—or who commit other types of
crimes. Rather, there is a collective washing of the hands, as if to concede
that heroes are no longer pure and little can be done to change that.

Unfortunately, this approach is unacceptable due to the growing
numbers of youth and younger children who look to male athletes as
examples. Whether or not choosing an athlete as a role model is good
judgment, kids have nonetheless elected them as their heroes. Thus, there
must be more willingness on the part of teachers, parents, youth-league
coaches, and other adults to resist patronizing criminally abusive athletes.
The forgive-and-forget, boys-will-be-boys approach cannot be tolerated.
Until the public demonstrates their disdain for high-profile males who
violate women, incidents of sexual assault by athletes will only increase.

References

Athlete's high salaries. (1993, August 23). *USA Today,* p. C1.

Barkley, C., & Johnson, R. (1992). *Outrageous.* New York: Simon & Schuster.

Barnett makes most of second chance. (1994, January 9). *The Kansas City Star,* p. C10.

Benedict, J. (1997, May 9). Colleges must act decisively when scholarship athletes run afoul of the law. *The Chronicle of Higher Education,* p. B6.

Benedict, J., & Klein, A. (1997). Arrest and conviction rates for athletes accused of sexual assault. *Sociology of Sport, 14,* 86-94.

Berkow, I. (1992, February 25). A champ named Desiree. *The New York Times,* p. D1.

Berkowitz, A. (1992). College men as perpetrators of acquaintance rape and sexual assault: A review of recent research. *The Journal of American Health, 40,* 175-181.

Blum, D. (1995, February 24). All part of the game. *The Chronicle of Higher Education,* p. A39.

Borges, R. (1992, January 26). Trouble follows Tyson. *The Boston Globe,* p. 53.

Bozworth, B., & Reilly,. R. (1988). *The Boz: Confessions of a modern anti-hero.* New York: Doubleday.

Brubaker, B. (1994, November 13). NFL teams support Perry despite past. *The Washington Post,* p. A25.

Chamberlain, W. (1992). *A view from above.* New York: Penguin.

Converse steps up third-place effort. (1995, March 2). *USA Today,* p. B1.

Crosset, T., Benedict, J., & McDonald, M. (1995). Male student-athletes reported for sexual assault: A survey of campus police departments and judicial affairs offices. *The Journal of Sport and Social Issues, 19,* 126-140.

Declination report, case no. 95-29998. (1995, August). County of La Crosse, Wisconsin, Office of the District Attorney.

Dershowitz, A. (1993, May). The rape of Mike Tyson. *Penthouse Magazine,* p. 58.

Estrich, S. (1987). *Real rape*. Cambridge, MA: Harvard University Press.

Fainaru, S., & Murphy, S. (1993, January 14). Webb case still murky. *The Boston Globe*, p. 35.

Farrey, T. (1993a, March 27). Bengals accuser tells of trauma after alleged rape. *The Seattle Times*, p. B1.

Farrey, T. (1993b, April 8). Woods says Victoria C. blackmailed Bengals—players deny rape, assault. *The Seattle Times*, p. G3.

Fila steps up U.S. marketing effort. (1995, January 13). *USA Today*, p. 3B.

Garrison, G., & Roberts, R. (1994). *Heavy justice: The state of Indiana v. Michael G. Tyson*. Reading, MA: Addison-Wesley.

Gorov, L. (1993a, March 18). 2d woman accuses Celtics' Webb of attacking her. *The Boston Globe*, p. 1.

Gorov, L. (1993b, March 28). Ex-Celtic ponders future as legal troubles unfold. *The Boston Globe*, p. 18.

Gorov, L. (1993c, March 28). Webb's past offers glimpse of man part brat, teddy bear. *The Boston Globe*, p. 1.

Horovits, B. (1995, January 27). Will viewers stay tuned or hit kitchen. *USA Today*, p. B1.

Hudson, D. (1993). Matching athlete and image: Learning a lesson from Tanya Harding. *Pro Sports Business Journal, 1,* p. 3.

Investigation summary. (1995, August). County of La Crosse, Wisconsin, Office of the District Attorney.

Investors bullish on Jordan's return. (1995, March 14). *USA Today*, p. 1.

Johnson, E., & Novak, W. (1992). *My life*. New York: Ballantine.

Koss, M., & Gaines, J. (1993). The prediction of sexual aggression by alcohol use, athletic participation and fraternity affiliation. *Journal of Interpersonal Violence, 8,* 94-108.

Koss, M., Gidycz, C., & Wisniewski, N. (1987). The scope of rape: Incidence and prevalence of sexual aggression and victimization in a national sample of higher education students. *The Journal of Consulting and Clinical Psychology, 55,* 162-170.

Langner, P., & Gorov, L. (1993, July 21). Webb pleads guilty to assault. *The Boston Globe*.

Massachusetts v. Marcus Webb, Case No. 93-00533 (1993).

Matoesian, G. (1993). *Reproducing rape: Domination through talk in the courtroom*. Chicago: The University of Chicago Press.

Messner, M., & Sabo, D. (1994). *Sex, violence and power in sports*. Freedom, CA: The Crossing Press.

Michael G. Tyson v. State of Indiana, The Brief of Appellant Michael J. Tyson, No. 49A02-9203-CR-129 (Ind. Ct. App. Sept. 18, 1992).

Mike Tyson speaks. (1994, Winter). *The Ring*, p. 39.

Nack, W. (1986, January 6). Ready to sour to the very top. *Sports Illustrated*, p. 23.

NFL's top dollars. (1995, January 18). *USA Today*, p. C1.

1994 NCAA division I graduation-rates report. (1994, June). Kansas City, KS: The National Collegiate Athletic Association.

Ozanian, M. (1993, May 25). Foul ball. *Financial World, 162,* p. 18.

Parrot, A., & Bechhofer, L. (1991). *Acquaintance rape: The hidden crime.* New York: John Wiley.

Pro football players join the licensing game. (1995, January 6). *USA Today,* p. B1.

Ranalli, R. (1993, March 19). Webb's woes mount. *The Boston Herald,*, p. 96.

Rhoden, W. (1995, January 10). For Deion, it must be the money. *New York Times,* p. D1.

Rodman, D. (1996). *Bad as I wanna be.* New York: Delacorte Press.

The rules of the game. (1993, November 12). *20/20* (transcript #1348) New York: ABC News.

Russell, D. (1984). *Sexual exploitation: Rape, child sexual abuse and workplace harassment.* Beverly Hills, CA: Sage.

Shaq attacks Shaq in new Reebok ads. (1995, January 18). *USA Today,* p. D1.

Shaughnessy, D. (1993, January 14). Caught in tangled web. *The Boston Globe,* p. 35.

Sherrington, K. (1994, October 2). Out of bounds: Experts debate connection between sport, violence against women. *Dallas Morning News,* p. 1.

Super bowl ads: Battle of egos. (1995, January 13). *USA Today,* p. B2.

A tangled Webb. (1993, March 19). *The Boston Herald,* p. 1.

Vachss, A. (1993). *Sex crime: Ten years on the front lines prosecuting rapists and confronting their collaborators.* New York: Random House.

Victoria C. v. Cincinnati Bengals, Inc., et al., Defendants' Trial Brief No. C92-658 (June 5, 1992).

Victoria C. v. Cincinnati Bengals, Inc., et al., Order No. C92-658M (Feb. 19, 1993).

Victoria C. v. Cincinnati Bengals, Inc. et al., Second Amended Complaint for Damages and for Rescision No. C92-658 (Filed Sept. 4, 1992).

Victoria C. v. Cincinnati Bengals, Inc., et al., Trial Brief of Defendants, No. C92-658 (Feb. 24, 1993).

Victoria C. v. Cincinnati Bengals, Inc., et al., Trial Brief of Defendants Carter, Francis, Green, Price, Rembert, and Thomas, No. C92-658 (Filed under seal pursuant to protective orders dated June 5, 1992 and Feb. 24, 1993).

Warshaw, R. (1994). *I never called it rape: The Ms. report on recognizing, fighting, and surviving date and acquaintance rape.* New York: HarperCollins.

Index

About the Author

Jeffrey R. Benedict is the former re-search coordinator at Northeastern University's Center for the Study of Sport in Society. He is the author of *Public Heroes, Private Felons: Athletes and Crimes Against Women.* His articles have appeared in the *New York Times, Los Angeles Times,* and the *Chronicle of Higher Education,* and he has contributed to ESPN.

Benedict was the lead researcher on a sociological study examining college athletes and violence against women. Published results of this study appeared in the *Sociology of Sport Journal, Journal of Sport & Social Issues,* and *Violence Against Women.* He has appeared as an expert on crime and athletes for ABC News, CBS News, NBC News, and ESPN.

He earned his bachelor's degree in history from Eastern Connecticut State University and a master's degree in political science from North-eastern University. He is currently attending the New England School of Law in Boston and is a lecturer in the sociology department at North-eastern University.